RETIREMENT PLANNING

A Guide for Canadians

Bruce D. McCarley

KEY PORTER BOOKS

Canadian Cataloguing in Publication Data

McCarley, Bruce D.
  Retirement planning: A guide for Canadians

Includes index.
ISBN 1-55013-460-4

1. Retirees — Canada — Finance, Personal.
2. Retirement — Canada — Planning.   3. Retirement income — Canada — Planning. I. Title.

HG179.M33 1993   332.024'0565   C92-095704-8

Key Porter Books Limited
70 The Esplanade
Toronto, Ontario
Canada M5E 1R2

Typesetting: True to Type, Inc.
Printed and bound in Canada

93 94 95 96 5 4 3 2 1

Contents

ACKNOWLEDGEMENTS

My thanks to Richard Birch who collaborated with me on this book. Richard's knowledge and experience as a professional business writer were invaluable on this project. He was a critical force in reducing tax "jargoneze" to language that is readable, descriptive, and informative.

I would also like to acknowledge the valuable input of a team of tax professionals drawn from various Deloitte & Touche offices across Canada. A team approach is a fundamental component of the delivery of client services by Deloitte & Touche. My thanks to the following:

Chuck Burkett, Victoria, BC
Christina Diles, New Westminster, BC
Robert Hudson, Vancouver, BC
Donald Lum, Vancouver, BC
Bob Zimmerman, Hamilton, ON
Marian Holland, Toronto, ON
Anne Montgomery, Toronto, ON
Bill Sherman, Toronto, ON
Denis Manning, St. John's, NF

DISCLAIMER

The information and analysis contained in this book are not intended to substitute for competent professional advice. Planning your financial affairs to reduce the tax you pay is a complex process — one that is unique to your business. The material that follows is provided solely as a general guide to assist you in understanding the main income tax provisions you may use to minimize your tax burden. No action should be initiated without consulting your professional advisors.

List of Abbreviations

AMT	Alternative Minimum Tax
CCPC	Canadian-Controlled Private Corporation
CDIC	Canada Deposit Insurance Corporation
CNIL	Cumulative Net Investment Loss
CPI	Consumer Price Index
CPP	Canada Pension Plan
C/QPP	Canada or Quebec Pension Plan
DPSP	Deferred Profit Sharing Plan
DRPP	Designated Registered Pension Plan
EPSP	Employee Profit Sharing Plan
GAAR	General Anti-Avoidance Rule
IRA	Individual Retirement Account
LIF	Life Income Fund
OAS	Old Age Security
QPP	Quebec Pension Plan
RCA	Retirement Compensation Arrangement
RPP	Registered Pension Plan
RRIF	Registered Retirement Income Fund
RRSP	Registered Retirement Savings Plan
SDA	Salary Deferral Arrangement
YMPE	Yearly Maximum Pensionable Earnings

Chapter 1 — Getting Ready to Retire

Getting ready to retire today isn't as easy as it used to be. Gone are the days of the gold watch, a handshake, and a small pension. In the 1990s, we're retiring with much larger incomes from more sources, and we have many more options of how and when to receive that income. We have larger and more varied assets, most of which need some attention paid to them before and during retirement, and then upon or before death. We have more choices of where to retire and when. And our options for deciding what we want to do with our retirement years are virtually unlimited.

The generation approaching retirement today can expect to be much more comfortable than any in the past. But getting ready for retirement now is much more complicated and, by the same token, more demanding of careful planning than at any time in the past. It's vital that you begin that planning well before you leave the nine-to-five world behind. There are literally hundreds of issues that should be settled before you receive your last paycheque or sell the business that you've laboured so hard over these past decades.

- How and when do you want to receive your pension?
- How big will that pension be and will it be enough?
- What kind of benefits will follow you into retirement?
- What kind of benefits won't be there after you retire, and what arrangements do you need to make before you leave your employer or the business?
- Are your RRSPs (registered retirement savings plans) and other private savings large enough to supplement your other sources of retirement income?

- What kind of government support can you expect?
- Will your Old Age Security be clawed back through the tax system?
- What kinds of other government benefits are available and where will they be available?
- Will you continue to live in the same house you've been occupying for the past few years or decades?
- Will you begin to summer at the cottage, or winter in the sunny south, or do you plan to travel extensively?
- Should you begin to think more seriously about estate planning?
- Will you continue to work at something that generates some income during your retirement?
- If you run your own business, will you keep a hand in the operation or bow out of the business completely?

The questions go on and on. Life has become more complex, and it won't get any simpler until you've answered most of these questions, taken the time to implement a well-thought-out retirement planning program, and actually retire. We'll try to deal with most of these questions, or at least the ones that bear on your financial well-being both before and after you retire.

THE CORNERSTONES OF RETIREMENT

Despite the complexities of preparing for retirement, the financial side of finally getting out of the rat race still boils down to paying attention to the four traditional cornerstones of retirement:

- pension and other benefits of employment;
- private saving, including RRSPs;
- your home and any other real estate in which you spend time;
- government income and other support.

Pension plans are much more flexible today than they have ever been. You may be able to decide how much to receive, how much your spouse will receive should you die before he or she does, what degree of indexing you want your payments to have, and what kind of benefits to have available when your Old Age Security (OAS) and Canada/Quebec Pension Plan (C/QPP) kick in. You might even be able to delay receiving your pension for a few years, or transfer your entire benefit into an RRSP, which could give you more flexibility. And some company benefits, such as extended health care, perhaps life insurance, financial counselling, and even club memberships could follow you into retirement for a period.

Most of us have contributed to an RRSP by the time we reach retirement. In many cases, Canadians have built up six-figure tax-sheltered investments in these plans. And once the mortgage is paid off, it becomes easier to invest elsewhere. For some, especially the self-employed and those who do not have access to a company pension plan, these private savings form the bulk of retirement income.

Owning a mortgage-free home is exactly the same as adding a substantial amount to your monthly income, now or during retirement. As well, it's an investment, as is any other real estate that you might own, such as a cottage, a ski chalet, or the condominium in a southern clime. All contribute to a comfortable retirement and all are available to supplement your retirement income if necessary.

The federal government provides two main sources of income — Old Age Security that is universally available but could be taxed back should your income exceed a certain level, and the Canada/Quebec Pension Plan into which you contribute during your working years. Many provinces also provide certain other benefits to pensioners, including breaks on property taxes, free or subsidized prescriptions, and even subsidized transportation.

The quality of your retirement years depends on your making the most of these four cornerstones before you retire — in the five, ten, or fifteen years before you are finally out of the harness. These are the years when you have the resources, the flexibility, and the ability to look ahead with a fair degree of certainty. You owe it both to yourself and to your family to get all your retirement ducks in a row now. Scrambling to catch up in the few months before you retire or even after you retire can be a recipe for disaster.

You will retire. Very few of us work forever, and fewer want to these days. There are just too many things to do and places to see. Most of us will have the resources to fulfil our desires in the first years after we retire, but only if we plan properly and begin that planning now.

Chapter 2 — When Do You Want to Retire?

More and more Canadians are retiring early, that is, before the current accepted standard of age 65. Many employers offer incentives for early retirement in a bid to open up positions and advancement to the younger members of their workforce. The federal government allows you to begin receiving C/QPP as early as age 60, although OAS does not begin until age 65. And you can convert your RRSPs into a retirement income anytime before you turn 65.

Early retirement sounds tempting — just what many of us have been dreaming about — but it comes at a cost. Analysis after analysis has demonstrated that retiring in your fifties is beyond the financial capabilities of most workers. They simply have not accumulated enough resources in their relatively low-paid, relatively expenditure-heavy, and relatively few working years to accommodate many extra years of retirement.

- Pension benefits are generally based on your years of service and the size of your salary or wages. Without those extra years of service in your fifties and sixties, when you will be at your peak earning power, you will receive a much smaller pension than if you retire at age 65.
- While early contributions to an RRSP are certainly important, you'll be able to make your largest contributions in your fifties and sixties, when you are earning the most. Many workers rely on these contributions to provide a significant portion of the funding for their retirement because they were unable to make large contributions earlier when they were raising a family, accumulating assets, such as a home, and financing their children's education.

- Most workers simply do not have the cash available to make significant investments until they are in their fifties and sixties, when they finally find that they have some "spare" earnings. These investments also help to fund the retirement years of many Canadians.
- Most people don't fulfil the dream of paying off their mortgage until they hit their fifties. A mortgage-free home releases a great deal of cash that can be used for investing or contributing to your RRSP, both of which enhance your retirement.
- Similarly, most Canadians can't, for one reason or another, manage to be completely debt-free until they are well into their fifties. One of the most significant expenses you are likely to have in your forties and fifties is putting your children through university or college and then perhaps helping them get started on their own career or on their own home. Those still faced with such expenses generally won't have the resources available to consider an early retirement.

It's an unfortunate fact of life that your peak earning years occur between about ages 50 and 65. These are the years you put your financial house in order — pay off your debts, maximize your investments, and accumulate those assets that will follow you into retirement. These last ten or fifteen years can make a huge difference in how comfortably or uncomfortably you retire.

RETIRING EARLY MAY NOT BE IN THE CARDS

Let's look at a relatively uncomplicated example. Adam and Betty are both age 55 and have been married for many years. Their three children are grown, and all have now begun to pursue their careers. Adam currently makes $60,000 a year and has been with the same employer for 20 years. Betty, who was out of the workforce for a number of years raising the children, makes $30,000. They have no debts other than the mortgage on their home, the payments on which run about $15,000 a year. They remortgaged at a higher amount to finance their children's post-secondary education, so the mortgage will not be discharged for another five years.

Adam belongs to a pension plan at his place of employment. It's a defined benefit plan (see Chapter 5) and promises to pay him

1.5 per cent of the average of his best three years' income, times the number of years of pensionable service that he has accumulated with his employer. Betty has managed to accumulate $100,000 in her RRSP, much of which has come from spousal contributions made by Adam (see Chapters 8 and 10). She has no pension plan where she works. Adam has just started contributing to his own RRSP and both are now making maximum RRSP contributions each year.

For the purposes of the example, we'll assume that the after-tax earnings rate on investments is 6 per cent, inflation averages 2 per cent, and wage hikes average 4 per cent. The earnings rate on retirement income and retirement annuities is 8 per cent. Let's look at what Adam and Betty can look forward to if they retire now at age 55, age 60, and age 65. Please note that the numbers are approximations based on a variety of assumptions that may not reflect your current situation or conditions in the future.

Retire at Age 55

If Adam and Betty retire at age 55, they can expect only two sources of income to kick in immediately — Adam's pension and Betty's RRSP:

Adam's pension	$17,400
Betty's RRSP	8,580
Total retirement income	$25,980

This total of $25,980 is only 29 per cent of their current total income of $90,000. In fact, after paying taxes on it, they would just barely be able to cover their mortgage payments, which continue for another five years, and pay for food for a few months. Their CPP benefits won't kick in for another five years and OAS won't start until they turn age 65. Clearly, retirement now is out of the question.

Retire at Age 60

If Adam and Betty retire at age 60, they can look forward to three additional sources of income — CPP for both of them, and Adam's RRSP, to which he has been contributing for only the past five years:

Adam's pension	$26,330
Adam's RRSP	2,030
Adam's CPP	6,300
Betty's RRSP	16,080
Betty's CPP (½ Adam's)	3,150
Total retirement income	$53,890

In today's dollars, assuming an average inflation rate of 2 per cent, this translates into about $48,810, which is considerably better than the $25,980 they would receive if they retired at age 55. At age 55, Adam and Betty were earning $90,000, but about $25,000 came out of their income to finance their mortgage payments ($25,000 less tax of $10,000 at 40·per cent equals $15,000). The mortgage has been paid off, so we have assumed that the $15,000 after-tax is being invested for their retirement. Thus, they have pre-tax disposable income of about $65,000 in today's dollars, which is the number that should be compared with $48,810. In other words, if they retire at age 60, they would have about 75 per cent of their disposable pre-tax income still available ($48,810/$65,000).

This is certainly an improvement on the income that they would have if they retired at age 55 (29 per cent of retirement income to working income). However, retiring still means experiencing a significant drop in disposable income. Not having the mortgage helps, but their standard of living would definitely have to drop. If they continued to work, they would be much better off, especially considering that the mortgage is no longer a problem.

Retire at Age 65

If Adam and Betty wait until age 65 to retire, they will have a total of eight different sources of income — the five noted above if they retire at age 60, plus OAS that is paid to both of them, and income from investments that they have accumulated with the funds that used to go to making payments on their mortgage. We'll assume that they buy an annuity with the funds accumulated from investing. We'll also assume that Adam's OAS is reduced from the maximum because he is subject to the clawback (see Chapter 16).

Adam's pension	$ 38,450
Adam's RRSP	5,650
Adam's CPP	10,940
Adam's OAS (less $990 clawback)	4,370
Betty's RRSP	28,800
Betty's CPP (½ Adam's)	5,470
Betty's OAS	5,360
Investment annuity	8,150
Total retirement income	$107,190

This retirement income of $107,190 is worth about $87,900 in today's dollars. Compare that with the $65,000 they are earning today, after allowing for their mortgage payments. Their retirement income is about 135 per cent of their current income. That's certainly a handsome sum to look forward to, compared to the amount that supports their current standard of living.

The dollars are not the important factor in this example. If your family income is double or half that of Adam and Betty, simply adjust the numbers proportionately. What is important are the percentages, the jumps from retiring with 29 per cent of your income at age 55 to retiring with 75 per cent at age 60 to retiring with 135 per cent at age 65. That's how important those last ten years can be. Adam and Betty went from not even scraping by if they retired at age 55, to retiring extremely comfortably if they wait until age 65. And by waiting until age 65, they can build a reasonable degree of inflation protection into their retirement income and not see their standard of living drop, since their projected retirement income is 35 per cent higher than their earnings before retiring.

Of course, deciding when to retire and deciding how much is enough depends on your personal situation and a host of other factors, many of which you cannot control. Adam and Betty could conceivably have enough at age 60. Their OAS kicks in five years later and by being careful not to lead an extravagant retirement, they might be quite comfortable in their twilight years. The operative word here is "might". By retiring at age 60, they have no extra resources to build in any inflation protection and no real cushion should an emergency of any sort arise. The next chapter discusses how much is enough for Adam and Betty, and perhaps for you.

RETIRING SLOWLY

More and more Canadians are considering and then following through with an early "semi-retirement". They begin receiving some retirement income, but are still earning income from one source or another.

- Many employees either manage to work out an arrangement with their employers to slow down to perhaps two days a week, or work for a few days or weeks or months during the employer's busy period, or perhaps work on projects on a contract basis.
- Many people take the skills they have accumulated from their many years of employment and start a business that may or may not demand much of their time.
- Some people who retire are fortunate enough to have a hobby that, when pursued as a business, generates a fair amount of income. Others turn their eye to a completely different lifestyle that may generate considerably less income than when the person was employed, but that results in a great deal of satisfaction.
- Some people approaching retirement age buy into an existing business and get involved on their own terms.
- Many business owners either slowly bow out of their enterprises as they hand over the reins to their children, or may stay on in a part-time managerial role if they sell the business to outsiders.

In each case, being able to tap into some retirement income makes the change from full to partial involvement possible. Early semi-retirement becomes a possibility when reduced pensions are added to the income generated from these activities. As well, this part-time work allows you to continue to make RRSP contributions or perhaps stay involved with your company pension plan, so that when you finally quit work for good, your retirement income is not impaired.

There are, however, several drawbacks to becoming semi-retired. First, you are not allowed to draw on your C/QPP until you are either age 65, or, if you are between ages 60 and 65, substantially retired, which usually means that your work-related or business income in the 12 months after you begin to receive C/QPP benefits cannot exceed the amount of benefits that you receive. For most contemplating semi-retirement, that means waiting until age 65.

Second, you may not be able to draw from your company pension plan until you either are completely retired or have left the employ of the company. In any case, you will not be able to begin receiving an early pension until you are ten years or less away from normal retirement age as spelled out in your pension plan.

Both these factors mean that you may have to rely on your private savings and RRSP to supplement your semi-retirement income. Many people contemplating semi-retirement may want to do just that, leaving their government and company benefits to at least age 65 or later, when they retire completely.

If you are participating in a business, there is also a fair amount of risk involved with semi-retirement. Chances are you either are investing your savings in the business or the business represents a great deal of resources that will be used to generate retirement income. If your business plans don't work out or your business falls on hard times, you may be putting your entire retirement in jeopardy. By the time you are within striking distance of retiring, you ought to be conserving your assets and ensuring that you have enough to see you and your spouse through another few decades. This is not the time to be taking great risks with everything that you have fought for so long to build up.

Chapter 3 — How Much Is Enough?

Can you ever have too much income or savings available during your retirement years? Probably not. Who knows what the next 20 or 30 years hold in store for you and your savings, not to mention the economy or even the country. Still, getting to that enviable position may mean retiring much later than you want, or perhaps not even retiring at all.

However, you can certainly end up with too little. And too many Canadian workers are in exactly that situation. Recent surveys point out that surprisingly few workers are preparing adequately for retirement. They are not saving enough. They begin saving too late. They rely too heavily on government programs. And they have unrealistic expectations about when they can retire and how well-off they will be financially. Many of those who are actively trying to save for retirement aren't using the tax system to their best advantage.

Even more shockingly, many Canadians do not appear to realize that once they retire, they lose a great deal of control over how much income they can generate. While we are still working, we are usually promoted, receive yearly raises, generate more sales, look for other income opportunities, and often have a spouse working. In other words, up to a point, we can have considerable control over our incomes. Once retired, we lose that control. Pension income may be fixed for life with no annual increases, even though inflation may return to the double digit range that we saw in the 1970s and early 1980s. Government income is indexed, but OAS is now taxed back if your income is above a certain level. You may have some control over how you generate income from your savings, but you will probably still have to opt for conservative, secure returns, which means your income may not keep pace with changing times. Most workers should not plan on earning a substantial income once they retire. The realities of the workplace say this is unlikely, except in a few isolated circumstances, and most workers retire for one very specific reason — they want to stop working and enjoy themselves.

Bearing in mind that, at retirement, you will lose much of the income-earning flexibility that you now enjoy and that you will be dependent on the sources of retirement income that you establish now, it makes sense to accumulate as much as possible while you can, so that you will maximize your income during your retirement years.

WHAT DOES THE FUTURE HOLD?

How much you actually will need during those ten, twenty, thirty or more years of retirement depends on four primary factors:

1. Your financial needs the day you retire and subsequent to that time.
2. How long you, your spouse, and any other dependants will live.
3. The rate of inflation throughout the entire period of your retirement and the number of years any dependants may still be relying on your income.
4. The earnings potential of your savings that are to be used to generate retirement income.

None of these factors can be predicted with even a little bit of certainty, although you can take a reasonably informed stab at estimating your financial requirements immediately upon retirement. Probably the best way to approach this question is to examine your current spending patterns and make a variety of adjustments.

CHARTING THE FIRST YEAR

First, you'll certainly be able to get by on less, considerably less actually. By the time you retire, you should have paid off your mortgage, which was likely eating up a significant portion of your take-home income. You will also likely be finished with your retirement saving, whether through your employer or by private saving such as in RRSPs. Your work-related expenses should drop off to zero. Your children should no longer represent a drain on your income if they have finished school and are well-launched into their careers. And with any luck, you'll be finished with most of your big-ticket expenditures.

On the other side of the ledger, you will be facing a few additional expenses, most of them welcome. Since you'll have considerably more spare time at your disposal, you'll be spending more on leisure — perhaps a lot more. Many couples travel extensively in the first few years of retirement. And others buy a second or even a third property, or perhaps a large boat. In other words, retirement is often the time when many couples finally open their wallets to everything they have been denying themselves over the past few decades as they established themselves in their careers, raised a family, and began accumulating assets. Finally, you will be faced with additional expenses that relate to being older. A few government freebies, such as lower public transportation costs or help with prescription drugs, probably won't make up for increased costs of health care, higher insurance premiums, and expenses associated with your special needs as you age.

There is one sure thing — many of your expenses will decline as you get further and further into your retirement. Everybody slows down eventually, and after a few years you will have done and seen most of what you had your heart set on once you quit working. But when will you begin slowing down? And how much will you spend in those first years of retirement compared with later?

If your health remains good, your spending may not slow down for 20 years or longer. Then again, your health could slowly deteriorate in such a manner that you begin racking up large medical expenses quite soon after you retire, although this is becoming less and less likely. Canadians are living longer than they ever have and not experiencing serious health problems until much later in life.

HOW LONG WILL YOU LIVE?

A man retiring at age 65 today will live, on average, into his late seventies or early eighties. A woman will make it into her mid-eighties. It is not unusual for couples to survive into their nineties, and the odds are that one spouse will make it very close to ninety if both are in reasonably good health at age 65.

If you and your spouse retire in your early sixties and live until your early nineties, that's 30 years of retirement — just a few years short of the time you were in the work force. What that means is that for each week you worked, you have to have earned enough to finance one week of retirement. Presumably, if you are within striking distance of weighing anchor from the work force, you have taken care of a great deal of this funding. If you haven't, you face the daunting task of trying to put enough away over a few short years to last you for decades.

SOURCES OF INCOME

The average Canadian's retirement income is received from several different sources. Typically, pension benefits are guaranteed for life and generally will provide some kind of survivor benefit for your spouse. Life annuities that arise from pension or private saving also go on for life and can be arranged with survivor clauses. Government OAS and C/QPP benefits are guaranteed for life and the C/QPP has a guaranteed survivor benefit. However, unless you exercise care, your private saving and your RRSPs may not outlast you. You can, though, make arrangements for your savings and RRSPs to last a lifetime, although you will give up some flexibility in terms of how you receive income early on in your retirement.

It is extremely important that you look at the flow of income each source is likely to generate. With most, you now have considerable choice over when to receive the income and how much to receive now or later. It should be possible, for example, to arrange for an extra $10,000 or $20,000 to be received during the first few years of your retirement when you expect your spending to be at a peak, and then cut back on your receipts in later years.

FACTORING IN INFLATION

Putting together a program that satisfies your expected cash requirements over an unknown number of years is only one part of the retirement equation. Just as important are the two other big unknowns — how inflation will affect your income and spending during your retirement years, and how the earnings rate on your savings will affect the size of the income that can be generated.

The two unknowns more or less go hand in hand. Higher inflation generally means higher earnings rates on your savings, at least as far as interest and dividend rates are concerned. Low rates of inflation mean lower interest and dividend rates, although the ratios between earnings and inflation won't necessarily be the same. Still, high and low inflation can both be damaging, although low interest rates will be helpful if you still have a mortgage when you retire. Earning 14 per cent on your savings may sound attractive, but if your cost of living is going up by 10 per cent every year, you may find yourself falling further and further behind once taxes are factored in. Earning 6 per cent or 7 per cent may not be nearly as attractive, but if inflation stands at only 1 per cent or 2 per cent, at least you won't see the purchasing power of your after-tax dollars erode year by year. However, you may have a problem just making ends meet if you are relying on earning that 14 per cent each year to meet your basic expenses, but interest rates drop back to 6 per cent.

Generally, if you own your own home, have paid off your mortgage, have made your big expenditures, and have financed your children's education, high inflation rates may not be that much of a problem. Yes, you'll see the effects when you buy food, pay your utility bills, or put gas in the car, but you won't feel the truly severe effects of high inflation the way a younger couple with children would. However, your expenses will still increase substantially each year, and if a large portion of your retirement income is fixed, that is, it is not adjusted each year for increases in the cost of living, you could eventually run into problems. As noted, if inflation is low and much of your income depends on interest-bearing investments, you could also have a problem.

Thus, it is essential that you build as much inflation protection into your planned retirement income as possible. Government income is automatically indexed. Private saving can be indexed by using indexed annuities or simply by reinvesting a portion of your income and using only what you need. A variety of methods can be used to index RRSP retirement income. However, if you belong to an employer-sponsored pension plan, indexing may not be possible, although more and more plans are offering this as an option, with, of course, reduced benefits during your first few years of retirement. If your other indexed income may not provide sufficient protection, you might consider investing a portion of your pension income so that it is available in later years when inflation has taken its toll on your pension.

Whether you attempt to index your retirement income based on actual increases in the cost of living, which is possible in some cases, but could be prohibitively expensive, or simply index it by 3 per cent or 4 per cent a year, or whatever figure you feel comfortable with, you should begin investigating the possibilities at least a year before you retire. Some of the retirement income options, such as annuities, depend on current interest rates. If rates are expected to drop drastically, as they did throughout the first nine months of 1992, you could be better off locking in with an indexed annuity when rates are still high, even though you have to recognize a certain amount of income for tax purposes that you have no real need of immediately.

Adam and Betty Revisited

Let's revisit Adam and Betty, whom we met in the previous chapter. As you will recall, at age 65, their income at retirement was about 135 per cent of their income in the last year that they worked. However, of the $107,190 they would receive in retirement income at age 65, only $26,140 was indexed. This included only their OAS and C/QPP benefits. None of the income from Adam's pension, their RRSPs, and their investment annuity was indexed. This means that about 76 per cent of their income is not protected against inflation.

They can do something about this, but at a cost. First, let's assume that Adam's pension plan has an option under which he can choose to receive indexed benefits. However, if he chooses this option, his initial payments from the plan will be reduced, depending on how much indexing is chosen. Of course, the plan could also have no indexing feature and make level payments for the rest of Adam's life. Or the employer may at various points make *ad hoc* increases to the pension benefits to allow for inflation.

Second, Adam and Betty can choose to receive indexed annuities from their RRSPs, or they can convert their RRSPs into an RRIF (registered retirement income fund) and receive payments from the RRIF that are essentially indexed. Similarly, the investment annuity could be indexed.

In the example, we have assumed that inflation averages 2 per cent, so let's index all the income, except the government income, by 2 per cent. This means that their income in the first year after retirement drops to $94,400 from $107,190. Instead of retiring with 135 per cent of their final year's income, they now retire with 119 per cent (on a discounted basis). This is still a handsome sum, and with the indexing built in, it should satisfy them for all their retirement years.

If Adam and Betty think that 2 per cent indexing is not high enough, they will have to take a larger hit on their retirement income. For example, if they index all their income, except for the government income, at 4 per cent, their total income drops to about $82,800, which is only 104 per cent of their income in the year before they retired. Depending on their spending, their standard of living may or may not improve. Chances are, however, that they will no longer have as much to spend in the first few years of retirement as they had planned. They can look forward to a secure retirement, but not quite the one they expected.

PROTECTING AGAINST INTEREST RATE FLUCTUATIONS

It's much more difficult to protect yourself against interest rate fluctuations. It was not too long ago that GICs (guaranteed investment certificates) were earning 12 per cent and better. In late 1992, they bottomed out at 5 per cent and 6 per cent. Locking in for the long term at 12 per cent apparently would have been a good strategy late in 1991. However, it was only ten years ago that interest rates were approaching the 20 per cent range. If they hit that level again, 12 per cent may seem like 6 per cent today — pitifully small and, for many retirees, simply not adequate.

In other words, there is considerable risk in adopting just one strategy, especially if you are retired and no longer can control how you go about earning income. The safest route is to diversify and pursue a relatively conservative investment strategy. Diversifying includes:

- staggering the maturities of your fixed-income investments;
- purchasing your fixed-income investments from a variety of sources;
- purchasing your fixed-income investments in more than one currency;
- varying your portfolio among interest-bearing securities and equities;
- using mutual funds to achieve diversification if your portfolio is not large enough to achieve a healthy degree of diversity on its own;
- using several different mutual funds from different issuers;
- listening to as many different points of view on the economy and investment climate as possible;
- considering alternative investments, such as real estate, if your portfolio is relatively large;
- using professional investment managers whenever possible to ensure a diversity of opinion.

Unless your private savings are relatively large, you certainly won't be able to diversify enough so that most risk is eliminated. However, even those with minimal savings can diversify enough to minimize the negative impact of wild swings in the economy.

Balancing the need for growth in your investments against your personal financial needs will probably be a new experience for most retirees. Up to the time they retire, their investing has focused primarily on accumulation of capital, not generating a stream of income that may have to last 30 or 40 years. This and other topics are covered more thoroughly in Chapter 10.

Chapter 4 — Where Do You Want to Retire?

If you are like many Canadians who have just retired, you'll probably consider spending much of the year, including the summer months, in Canada, and spending a few months during the winter "down south". The Canadian home may be the family cottage or a West Coast home or even the old family home in the city, while you may spend the winter months in the southern United States or the Caribbean or in one of hundreds of other locales that provide a more hospitable winter climate than Canada.

WHERE TO RETIRE IN CANADA

Deciding where to retire in Canada generally boils down to personal preference and circumstance. Proximity to family tends to play a major role in the decision-making process. Climate may be another major factor — many Canadians opt for the West Coast, swearing that they just can't take another Canadian winter of the type that occurs east of the Rocky Mountains. Many Canadians are now choosing to retire at an earlier age than the previous generation, but continue part-time work on a consulting basis with their employer or stay involved with their business on a part-time basis. In these types of situations, staying where you are may be the most prudent option.

One of the attractions of British Columbia is its low provincial tax rate. It ranks fourth lowest behind the Northwest Territories, the Yukon, and Alberta. While few people consciously choose to retire in British Columbia rather than in their current province for tax reasons, it can make a difference. For example, if your taxable income is about $50,000 in 1992, you would pay about $1,400 less tax in British Columbia than if you retired in Manitoba, $750 less than in Nova Scotia, and about $150 less than in Ontario.

Estate planning considerations may also enter in when deciding whether to move to another province. For example, there are currently no provincial succession duties or gift taxes or any other type of death tax levied in Canada, other than the inescapable federal "death taxes", which are examined in some detail in Chapter 11. However, Ontario recently brought up the possibility of reintroducing succession duties, but so far has not pursued the matter. Hinting at a resumption of succession duty taxation certainly doesn't provide enough reason to remove yourself from Ontario or any other province. Governments change and new thinking comes along regularly.

Perhaps of more concern might be the current status of family law in your province of residence and the one to which you are contemplating moving. The rules for division of assets on the breakdown of a marriage and on the death of a spouse vary from province to province. For example, in Ontario, marital assets must be split evenly on divorce and special rules apply to the matrimonial home. Marital assets include virtually everything accumulated during the marriage, except for gifts made specifically to one spouse, and can include business assets as well as pension accumulations. Upon death, the surviving spouse can become entitled to one-half the marital assets if he or she is not entitled to them under the terms of the will of the deceased spouse. Similar rules apply in a number of other provinces, but not all. If these issues are a concern to you, you should definitely consult with a legal professional to determine where the law in a particular province currently stands.

There may be other financial considerations that you would have to take account of when deciding to retire out of province. The level of benefits, whether free or subsidized, that are provided to seniors varies considerably from province to province. These may either wipe out any tax advantages or add to them. The level of medical care might vary to some extent and each province has slightly different rules on coverage when you are out of the country. Moving to another province may also add to or reduce other costs, such as travel to see your family or to see the world. Housing may be more or less expensive, as might utilities and property taxes. If

WHERE DO YOU WANT TO RETIRE? 21

you come from a small town or the country, retiring in the city could prove to be much more costly than if you were to stay put.

Deciding where to retire in Canada may also influence where you spend your winter months down south. Arizona and California are obviously much closer and therefore much cheaper to visit than Florida if you are living on the West Coast. However, flights out of eastern cities to Florida in the winter months and accommodations there can be particularly inexpensive.

Moving across the country is expensive — certainly not the type of outlay you want to incur in the first year or two of your retirement. However, if you can make the move while still employed, or you make the move to take up a business or employment in the new city, any moving expenses incurred are likely to be deductible for tax purposes. In the ideal situation, you persuade your employer to transfer you a few months or even a year or two before you retire. Your employer picks up the entire cost of the move plus any related costs of relocating, including, for example, losses realized on the sale of your old residence or the added expense of buying a home in the new city where real estate is more valuable.

If you must pay the shot, most of your expenses will be deductible assuming that you continue working for your current employer at the new location, or you take up work or start a business at the new location. The moving expenses can be deducted against income earned at the new location only in the year of the move and the year immediately following.

The deductibility of moving expenses is important to keep in mind if you relocate upon retiring. For example, if you move out of your current area and go back to school, your moving expenses could be deductible against any scholarship or bursary income to which you become entitled. Keep in mind that when determining the deductibility of any moving expenses, you must, at the very least, move 40 kilometres or more and be closer to the employer, business, or school at the new location than you were at the old location.

Similarly, you might move from the city to the country to retire and begin pursuing a part-time business of some sort. Generally, your moving expenses should be deductible in the year of the move or the following year against the business income generated at the new location, even though you might operate the business out of your home and sales from the business might be concentrated in the city you just moved from.

IS IT CHEAPER IN THE CITY OR THE COUNTRY?

More and more urban dwellers are choosing to retire in the "country" rather than remain in their city homes. "Country" in this case could be roughly defined as being anywhere but the city. It might be a smaller town on the outskirts of the city, a country retreat within a comfortable drive of the city, or a winterized cottage or farm property that has been owned for decades and is two or three hours from the urban centre. Some people might choose to truly get away from it all and move to a rural area far from the city.

Generally, as you move farther and farther away from large urban centres, real estate prices begin to decline, often drastically. But will your expenses decline as well? It all depends on your lifestyle and buying habits. If you retain your membership at the golf club and play three or four times a week, but it now takes an hour and a half to drive there, your gas bills are going to shoot way up. If you enjoy movies, the theatre, dining, gourmet food, and all the entertainment big cities have to offer, your monthly expenses may start to include extra gas for the car, plus more wear and tear on it, the occasional hotel room for overnight stays, and perhaps even more expenditures as you treat yourselves to "city delights" that just aren't available in the country.

Country life isn't for everyone. Many of us take city amenities for granted and are appalled to discover that life in the country doesn't include many of these "necessities". You might want to consider looking before you leap. Perhaps renting a country place for a year, while you rent out your city home, will reveal many of the advantages and disadvantages of country versus city living. You may discover that what you really want is a compromise. Or perhaps you really want to live in two or three different places during the year and also travel extensively. Committing yourself to a real estate purchase before trying out the new lifestyle can be particularly expensive if you change your mind a year later. And this expense may come when you can least afford it and no longer have the income-earning capability of making up for mistakes.

Chapter 5 — Where Do You Stand with Your Pension Plan?

What has your pension plan done for you lately? That's not such an odd question. Yes, your pension plan is designed, in theory, to provide a steady stream of income once you retire. But it's what has happened to the plan since you joined that determines how well you will fare during your retirement years.

The kinds of questions you might want to ask of your plan, or actually your employer or the plan's administrator, depend on the type of plan to which you belong and from which you can expect benefits.

TYPES OF PLANS

Defined Benefit Registered Pension Plan. For these types of plans, the pension benefit to be received at retirement is spelled out in the plan. The employer is responsible for contributing sufficient amounts today to fund the benefits promised for tomorrow. Employee contributions may be made, but generally the employer must fund at least half the benefit.

Defined Contribution Registered Pension Plan. The employer and, depending on the terms of the plan, the employee, contribute according to a formula each year, generally based on the employee's wages and perhaps years of service. At retirement, the best pension possible is purchased with the accumulated funds.

Deferred Profit Sharing Plan (DPSP). Contributions are made by the employer (employees cannot contribute to a DPSP) based on profits earned by the company. The contributions for a particular employee are based on that employee's wages and length of service. Benefits paid at retirement depend on the accumulations credited by the plan to the employee.

Group Registered Retirement Savings Plan. These are simply RRSPs to which contributions are made out of the employee's wages. However, the employer directs the employee's contributions to the plan. Like other RRSPs, the best pension possible is purchased at retirement, although currently, most group RRSPs do not have the many flexible retirement options offered by a regular RRSP.

Retiring Allowance. These are usually paid at retirement as a lump sum in lieu of or in addition to a pension. Guidelines are imposed by Revenue Canada for the deductibility of retiring allowances to the employer. For the retiring allowance to be fully deductible by the employer, it must be reasonable in the circumstances in relation to the employee's wages, length of service, and access to other company-sponsored retirement benefits.

Designated Registered Pension Plan. These are very similar to defined benefit RPPs, except they are for the benefit of significant shareholders of smaller businesses. Certain additional restrictions apply to these types of plans.

Non-registered plans and other types of arrangements that provide for additional retirement benefits or compensation are discussed in the next chapter.

How and when you receive benefits from these various retirement plans depends on the terms of the plan and, of course, your own particular needs. You will likely have the least flexibility or choice with a defined benefit RPP. However, since the method of calculating retirement benefits is spelled out for you exactly in a defined benefit plan, you should know approximately how much you will be receiving several years before retirement.

With the other types of plans, you do not know the size of your benefit until you actually begin receiving it, and then the benefit is usually received in the form of an annuity. Thus, it is dependent on interest rates in effect at the time your accumulations in the plan are converted to an annuity. Interest rates recently hit 20-year lows, which means that pension benefits have also declined. While inflation may also be at a 20-year low, the increased purchasing power that you may expect from your pension income may not offset the lower benefits that will become payable under some plans at a time when interest rates are low.

It is essential that you investigate the benefits that are offered under your particular plan and also explore what other options you might have either to increase your benefits, or perhaps delay them until interest rates begin moving upward again. In many cases, this may mean transferring your accumulated pension benefits to an RRSP when you retire, leaving the funds in the RRSP to grow for a number of years, and then arranging what you hope will be a much more attractive retirement income. Of course, you also will have to have a steady stream of income on which to live during those years. Depending on the terms of your plan, you may be able to choose to receive only a portion of your accumulated retirement benefits and transfer the rest to an RRSP. You should bear in mind that there is some risk involved in waiting for interest rates to increase. If inflation stays at its current levels, rates may actually decline further.

DEFINED BENEFIT REGISTERED PENSION PLANS

Most workers belong to defined benefit RPPs, and most of these workers know very little about their plans. Chances are good that you will receive more retirement income from your defined benefit RPP than from any other source. It makes sense that you should know as much about the plan as possible and know how you can take best advantage of the opportunities offered under the terms of the plan. The place to start is with the description and terms of the plan that you received when you first joined, and all the updates you have received since then, as well as your annual statements from the plan.

How Much Can You Expect to Receive?

Most plans issue annual statements that project how much you will receive in annual benefits from the plan, based on a number of assumptions. The primary benefit is based on your years of pensionable service and your wages. The maximum pension benefit that can be paid is the lesser of:

- $1,722.22 times each year of pensionable service, or
- 2 per cent times the average of your best three consecutive years of remuneration times the number of years of pensionable service.

The dollar maximum of $1,722.22 will be indexed to increases in the average wage after 1995.

The benefits that you can expect from your plan depend primarily on two factors:

- how your wages or salary will behave in the future until you retire, and
- how many years of pensionable service you will accumulate under your pension plan.

Most people expect their wages to go up faster than increases in the Consumer Price Index, which measures inflation. And most people expect to be promoted periodically, which will also act to increase their salary or wages over time. The question you must ask is, will this continue to be the case as you get close to retirement age? Will you be passed over for promotion and will you have to fight just to keep your wages or salary in line with inflationary increases?

To receive the maximum pension allowed, you must remain with the same employer throughout your working life, or at least remain under the same plan. If you take an early retirement, you will obviously be cutting into your years of service, which means you will likely receive a smaller pension. If you work for a number of employers over your career and belong to several different pension plans, you will also likely have fewer years of service and smaller benefits. The way the accumulation of benefits works and how these benefits are transferred between plans prejudices those who do not stay with one employer throughout their careers. Every time you leave one plan and attempt to take your accumulated benefits with you to another plan, you will lose a certain number of years of pensionable service, assuming that the two plans offer similar benefits. You generally will be eligible to "buy" additional years of service to make up for the lost ones, but under the new pension rules introduced several years ago, this may be impossible if you maximized your

RRSP contributions each year. The only solution is to transfer RRSP funds to your new plan to buy the additional years of service (*see below*). It is essential that you know how many years of service you have accumulated and whether you are eligible to buy additional years.

When thinking about how much retirement income you are likely to receive, it's safest to think in terms of percentages, not absolute amounts. For example, if your plan promises to pay you 2 per cent of the best average three years of salary, times each year of pensionable service, and you have 30 years, you should, on retiring, replace about 60 per cent of the income you were earning in the year before you retired. Then it's a simple matter of calculating how much of the slack will be taken up by government benefits, RRSP retirement income, and your other private savings.

If the terms of your plan are particularly complex, you might seek the aid of your employer's human resources department. For instance, your plan may be based on career average earnings, not on the best three or five years. Most people probably have no idea what their average yearly wages or salary to date might be. With 30 years of service, would your plan replace 50 or 40 or even only 30 per cent of your wages or salary in the year before you retire?

If your projections, or your employer's, show a shortfall, you should definitely begin exploring alternative methods of augmenting your retirement saving. There may be opportunities available under your current plan, or you may want to use RRSPs. As well, you may be able to negotiate for additional benefits from your employer.

Can You Buy Additional Benefits Under Your RPP?

Many plans permit members to buy additional benefits for years of service when they were not members of the plan, but were employed by the plan sponsor. The employer may or may not contribute toward the purchase of benefits for years before 1989. For benefits accruing for years of service after 1988, the employer generally must fund half the benefits that will eventually be paid out.

As well, you may be able to buy "upgrade" benefits. For example, your pension plan may have been upgraded to offer better benefits on retirement. However, employees have to buy into these upgrades. You should review any past upgrades to your plan and see whether you are entitled to acquire these additional benefits now or sometime in the future before you retire.

A variety of tax rules limits the amount that can be contributed to a defined benefit RPP and hence the additional retirement benefits that can be purchased. For pre-1989 benefits, the Income Tax Act placed limits on how much you were able to deduct from income each year in respect of your contribution to the RPP. For years after 1988, limits are placed on the amount of retirement benefits that can be purchased. The limit is tied in with how much you have contributed to your RRSP since 1989 and with benefits that you have earned from other retirement plans. For example, if your plan was upgraded three years ago and you made maximum RRSP contributions during those years, your ability to purchase these additional benefits today will be restricted, although there is a mechanism for removing funds from your RRSP or transferring them to your company pension plan to fund the additional benefits.

Your employer or pension plan administrator should be able to determine exactly how much you can contribute for additional benefits and how much will be deductible for tax purposes in a particular year. However, this area can be extremely complex, so you might want to confirm the numbers with your own tax advisor.

Does Your RPP Offer Inflation-Protected Benefits?

More and more pension plans are offering some form of inflation-protected benefits. Retirement benefits may be indexed at a specified percentage each year, or perhaps they keep pace with a certain percentage of the average annual increase in the Consumer Price Index. Other plans may offer *ad hoc* periodic increases to the level of benefits being paid. Unfortunately, these types of increases, if not mandated in the pension plan itself, tend to depend on the health and good fortunes of the employer, since it is the employer, not the trustees or the administrator of the plan, that pays the additional benefits.

Inflation protection might be an additional benefit that you can buy under your plan, or it might be available on retirement if you accept a smaller benefit in the year you retire.

As you'll recall from our discussion of the effects that inflation can have on retirement income in Chapter 3, it is crucial that you provide some type of inflation protection in your total retirement income package. Your government benefits, such as those from the C/QPP or the OAS, will be indexed, but if your RPP benefits are not, you should plan on ensuring that your RRSP or other savings generate some kind of indexed retirement income. Yes, inflation has, in the early 1990s, been wrestled to the ground. That's also what everyone thought in the 1960s, except that did not prove to be the case in the 1970s and 1980s. One of the goals of your retirement planning should be to inflation-proof as much of your retirement income as possible. The place to start is with what will likely be your largest source — your pension plan.

What Are Your Options on Retirement?

In most provinces, defined benefit RPPs are required to provide a benefit in a particular manner, depending, of course, on your pension entitlements. For example, if you are married, your plan must provide for a joint and last survivor benefit. This means that a certain percentage of your pension, usually at least 50 per cent, must continue to be paid to your spouse for his or her life should you die first. A variety of combinations might be available using different survivor percentages and guaranteed payouts to other dependants. Generally, both you and your spouse must elect in writing to receive a benefit other than the standard one.

Choosing the best way to receive your benefits should not be left to the last minute. The choices have many implications and the choice you make may affect how you deal with your other sources of retirement income. For example, you may opt to ensure that 100 per cent of the benefits of your pension continue to be paid to your spouse upon your death. Since this type of RPP benefit package costs more than the standard benefit that pays 60 per cent, the retirement benefits that you will receive will be lower. This may mean that you will have to dip into your RRSP sooner than expected to augment your retirement income, which in turn means that you may have to adjust your investment mix in your RRSP today to ensure that enough money is available at the time you retire to fund the additional income needs.

Are Your Pension Benefits Protected?

Most, but not all, pension plans are administered or trusteed by insurance companies, trust companies, or other entities. In other words, the contributions and earnings in the plan are not under the direct control of your employer. What this means is, should your employer experience financial difficulty, it should not be able to gain access to those pension assets. If the insurance or trust company trustee/administrator gets into any kind of financial problems, the pension assets should be segregated and protected from any shrinkage. As well, the insurance industry has a well-developed set of checks and balances to gauge the financial health of its members and it has also established a large fund to protect anyone adversely affected by an insurance company that does get into trouble.

Can You Take Your Pension Benefits Elsewhere?

Under pension reform, plans in most provinces must have some degree of portability — that is, you must be able to move the accumulated benefits to another RPP or to an RRSP. How portable the benefits in your plan prove to be ultimately depends on the terms of your plan. Portability also depends on the terms of the plan to which you are making the transfer. For example, assume that you change jobs and want to transfer your benefits to the plan of your new employer. You had accumulated 20 years of benefits under your old plan, but under the terms of your new plan, which is more generous, those 20 years of service translate into only 17 years of benefits. However, in most cases, all your years of service will be recognized, so you will be given the option of buying an additional three years under the new plan.

As well, because of the way pension plans calculate their future pension liabilities, it is unlikely that you will be able to transfer your benefits from one plan to another completely intact. For example, assume that you have 20 years of service with employer A and then you work your last 10 years before retiring at age 65 with employer B. Both employers sponsor identical plans that offer 2 per cent of your best average three years, times your years of service. When you leave employer A, your benefits are based on you retiring in year 30 at age 65, but your benefits are based on 20 years of service times 2 per cent of your average salary in years 18, 19, and 20. However, employer B is projecting those benefits that you want to transfer to fund a pension based on you retiring at the end of year 30, so your average salary in years 28, 29, and 30 forms the basis of the benefits. This pension requires considerably more funding than the one that employer A will eventually pay you at age 65. Even though the plans are identical, the cash transferred from plan A to plan B will not fund all 20 years of service. For instance, it may fund only 16 years of service under plan B and you will be given the opportunity of "buying" benefits for the additional four years. If you fund these years personally and they relate to years of service before 1990, you should be able to deduct your contributions at the rate of $3,500 a year until the amount deducted is exhausted. If they relate to years after 1989, your ability to buy those years of service depends on how much you have contributed to your RRSP in those years.

PRACTICAL POINTER If you are unable to contribute a significant amount to buy years of past service in your pension plan for years after 1988, consider transferring amounts from your RRSP to the plan to buy those past years of service. In most situations, your employer must finance at least half the benefits that are eventually payable for the past service years, so it will usually be worthwhile making the transfer.

If you transfer the cash value of your benefits to a money purchase or defined contribution plan (*see below*) or to an RRSP, the amount transferred will likely be much less than is actually needed to fund the type of retirement benefits that you were expecting.

As you get closer to retirement and build up years of service with your current employer, you will, like many others, likely find the golden handcuffs tightening up perceptibly every so often. If you are looking forward to retirement, this may not present itself as a problem; rather, it's your reward for long and faithful service to the same employer for many years. If you plan to put off retirement for many years and are looking for new challenges that are not available with your current employer, the emphasis will be on "handcuffs" and not on "golden". Moving to another job could involve so much cost in terms of forgone benefits that you would not be likely to recoup it given your age, the number of remaining employable years, and your current income level.

Note that if you are within ten years of the normal retirement age as stated in your plan, you can generally opt to leave your pension with the RPP of your old employer and begin receiving the benefits later when you retire. This may be preferable to transferring your benefits to another plan.

What Early Retirement Options Are Offered by Your Plan?

Most plans offer some type of early retirement option. Usually, your benefits will be scaled down depending on how many months or years you retire before the normal retirement date as stated in your plan. The terms can be extremely generous if your employer is trying to make room for the advancement of younger employees or is going through a downsizing phase. Or the terms may be decidedly unattractive.

If you are considering early retirement, you might want to consider having your independent financial advisor review the options under the plan and take a look at your other finances to determine how viable early retirement really is. Take the time to review the Adam and Betty example presented in Chapter 2.

Have You Reached the Maximum Pension Limit?

As noted above, a cap is put on the maximum pension benefit that can be paid in the first year you retire. For example, if you have 30 years of service under the plan, the maximum pension benefit you can receive today is $1,722.22 times 30 years, or $51,666 a year. This benefit can be indexed to increases in the cost of living.

Generally, if your salary exceeds $86,111 a year, you could be bumping up against the maximum allowable pension benefit, assuming this is what is promised under the terms of your plan. At this salary level, you and your employer will be contributing the maximum deductible amount allowed to the plan, which is the amount necessary to fund the maximum pension payable. At the same time, you will be permitted to make a deductible contribution to your RRSP of up to $1,000. No further amounts may be effectively contributed by you or your employer to tax-sheltered retirement plans and be deducted from income for income tax purposes. In fact, if contributions are made to registered retirement plans in excess of the amounts allowed under the Income Tax Act, severe consequences can arise for you, your employer, and the plan.

However, as explained in the next chapter, other opportunities may be available for generating additional retirement income for those whose salaries exceed the $86,111 threshold.

DEFINED CONTRIBUTION REGISTERED PENSION PLANS

Defined contribution RPPs have become more popular as the cost of operating a defined benefit plan has increased substantially over the past few years. Defined contribution, or money purchase plans as they are also called, are easy to operate, easy to understand,

and risk-free from the employer's point of view. Contributions are made each year, and the pension benefits depend on how well the plan performs over the working life of the employee. The only onus on the employer is to make the contributions and choose an administrator or trustee who can manage the contributions to the employee's best advantage. There is no requirement for the employer to make additional contributions to the plan if it does not perform well. In fact, some plans are now even transferring the investment decisions to the employees. They can choose what kinds of investments the administrator will make with their contributions, from extremely low-risk to relatively aggressive.

Limits apply to how much can be contributed to a defined contribution RPP each year and be deducted from income for tax purposes. In 1993, the limit is based on a contribution equal to 18 per cent of the employee's earnings in the current year, but only to a maximum of $13,500. The maximum jumps to $14,500 in 1994 and $15,500 in 1995. After 1995, it is proposed that the limit is to be indexed to increases in the average industrial wage. In most provinces, employers are required to make at least 50 per cent of the contributions to the plan. Note that both the employee and employer contributions are used in determining if the allowable limits are met or exceeded.

How Well Is Your Defined Contribution RPP Performing?

Since the size of your retirement benefits ultimately depends on how much your and your employer's contributions to the plan earn over the years that you are a member, it is crucial that you know how well your plan is performing. This information should be readily available from your employer, or perhaps the administrator of the plan, preferably on a quarterly basis.

If you belong to one of the newer, flexible defined contribution RPPs wherein you can determine your own investment mix, you may have to make an investment decision each time you review your plan's performance. This will be much the same exercise that those with self-administered RRSPs go through. For example, you may be able to direct a certain portion of your credits in the plan to one or more different types of investments or investment funds, ranging from very conservative (perhaps investing only in short-term government-backed securities) to relatively speculative (investing in equities, much like many of the hundreds of equity mutual funds).

In fact, your pension administrator might well be a mutual fund, a trust company with its own funds, or an insurance company with access to a number of different types of segregated funds (the insurance industry's term for its investment funds).

Investment counsellors generally say that the closer you are to retirement age, the less risk you should be taking with your retirement saving, which in this case includes the benefits you can expect to receive from a defined contribution RPP. Unfortunately, in the early 1990s, interest rates have taken a dive, which makes bonds and similar investments relatively unattractive, while the stock market's performance has been relatively lack-lustre over the past five or six years. Choosing a proper, or even a reasonable mix for your investments in your pension plan is not as easy as it once was, nor as easy as your employer possibly thought when the plan was instituted.

Can You, and Perhaps Your Employer, Increase Your Contributions?

The maximum annual contribution allowed to a defined contribution RPP that is deductible for tax purposes is 18 per cent of your employment earnings from your employer.

PRACTICAL POINTER If your RPP happens to be performing well and you and/or your employer are contributing less than the maximum, you might want to investigate the possibility of making additional contributions to the RPP rather than to your RRSP. To ensure that your employer continues to fund a portion of your pension benefit, your employer may also have to increase its contributions to the plan. If your employer is reluctant, you may be able to negotiate these higher employer contributions in lieu of a salary increase. Both amounts are deductible to the employer. In fact, the amount the employer contributes to the RPP may cost less than additional salary since there are no fringe benefits attached to the amount.

Bear in mind, however, that you generally have much less flexibility with a defined contribution RPP than you do with an RRSP. The retirement income options are much more restrictive and you may not have any control over them when you eventually opt to begin receiving your pension. As well, you may have little control over the investments in the plan. You might have the option of transferring your accumulated contributions and earnings to a locked-in RRSP (*see below*), but again, your retirement income options will be restricted.

What Are Your Pension Benefit Options?

Like defined benefit plans, defined contribution RPPs must offer a pension for life to the employee, with a surviving spouse benefit attached. The exact type of benefit that you do receive is generally dependent on what is available in the marketplace at the time you retire. However, your plan may be required to buy its pension benefit from the trustee or administrator of the plan, for instance, a life insurance company.

Your benefit will essentially be a life annuity and therefore must be issued by a life insurance company. This life annuity could be indexed, have 100 per cent survivor benefits, and/or have a guarantee period attached to it. For example, the benefits may be guaranteed to be paid for ten or fifteen years to your heirs should both you and your spouse die before the guarantee period expires. Keep in mind, though, that each bell and whistle you add to the basic retirement package (which is generally a pension for life for you, and a survivor benefit amounting to 60 per cent of your retirement benefit), reduces the amount of your monthly retirement payments.

You may also have the option of transferring your accumulated pension benefit as a lump sum into a locked-in RRSP. Whether this will improve your benefit options depends on the province in which you live. In Quebec, for example, amounts from a locked-in RRSP can be transferred to what is generally referred to as a "life income fund". These operate much like registered retirement income funds (RRIFs — see Chapter 8), except all amounts remaining in the fund must be transferred to a life annuity by the time the annuitant turns 80. Several other provinces have, or are considering introducing, similar plans. As well, the federal government intends to introduce legislation that would permit the direct transfer of RPP benefits to an RRIF, rather than the benefits having first to go into an RRSP. Since pension benefits are generally under provincial jurisdiction, each province would have to approve such transfers.

DEFERRED PROFIT SHARING PLANS (DPSPs)

DPSPs are popular with some employers for two primary reasons: contributions are made on the employees' behalf only when the company shows a profit, and the contributions can be invested in shares of the employer, provided the shares are a qualified investment. If the shares and other investments perform well, DPSPs can be popular with employees as well. Generally, the employer can contribute up to 18 per cent of the employee's wages to the DPSP, to a maximum of $6,750 in 1993 (rising to $7,250 in 1994, $7,750 in 1995, and indexed thereafter), which is half the maximum that can be contributed to a defined contribution RPP.

However, employees are not always enamoured of DPSPs for the same two reasons that they are often popular. In years when their employer is not performing well and little, if anything, is contributed to the DPSP, RRSPs are generally their only recourse to tax-assisted retirement saving. Of course, their employer likely does not compensate them for these RRSP contributions. And if the shares of the employer do not perform particularly well, the employees' eventual retirement benefits will suffer accordingly. As well, the employer's contributions to the DPSP eat into how much the employees can contribute to their RRSPs. So, if the DPSP performs poorly, the employees do not have the chance to make up for these lost earnings inside the tax-sheltered environment of an RRSP that may outperform the DPSP.

Opting out of your DPSP may be possible, but perhaps not that desirable. After all, the employer is making contributions to the plan on your behalf. Your wages do not suffer when contributions are made. If you choose to opt out, your only option may be to make RRSP contributions out of your current wages. In years when no DPSP contributions are made, you will not notice any difference in the level of your retirement saving since you would have made the RRSP contribution in any case. However, in years when the employer makes contributions to the DPSP, you lose out on those benefits and still must use your own funds for your RRSP contribution.

How Well Is Your DPSP Performing?

As you approach retirement age, it is vital that you monitor the performance of your DPSP. If the plan is invested solely in the securities of your employer, you essentially have a great deal of your retirement income eggs in one basket. If the value of the employer company takes a nosedive, your retirement benefits plummet right along with it. On the other hand, if the employer is a thriving company that is making healthy profits and is successfully expanding, your DPSP benefits could end up being much larger than you otherwise expected or than could be generated using an RRSP.

What Are Your DPSP Retirement Options?

Generally, your DPSP retirement options are extremely flexible. You can receive everything in your DPSP as a lump sum when you retire, and pay the tax, more than likely at the top rate for most of the amount received. You can also opt to receive a ten-year annuity or a life annuity with the amount.

PRACTICAL POINTER   Note that DPSP amounts can be transferred directly into an RRSP. You can then either take advantage of the extended tax deferral in the RRSP until age 71, or choose one of the several RRSP retirement income options (see Chapter 8). This last option gives you the most flexibility and lets you delay receiving your retirement for as long as the year after you turn age 71.

GROUP RRSPs

Group RRSPs have become much more prevalent over the last decade as it becomes more and more expensive for employers to sponsor registered pension plans. From the employer's point of view, group RRSPs are extremely simple to administer and inexpensive, and the costs to the employer are predictable from year to year. Most importantly, they are not subject to the new pension reform rules that affect RPPs. For example, there is no requirement that the employer fund half the pension benefits that are expected from the group RRSP.

Group RRSPs operate almost exactly the same as individual RRSPs (see Chapter 8 for a full discussion of RRSPs). A portion of your salary is contributed periodically to the group RRSP and you are entitled to deduct this amount from income for tax purposes. Depending on the terms of the plan, your employer may, in effect, make contributions on your behalf. However, since employers are not permitted to make contributions to group RRSPs (or individual RRSPs for that matter), the contribution is first recognized as an increase in your salary and then is contributed to the group RRSP. This "additional" salary is, of course, included in your income in the year the contribution is made, but is offset by the deduction allowed for the amount contributed to the group RRSP.

Group RRSPs should be differentiated from "locked-in RRSPs". This latter type is used when funds are transferred from an employer-sponsored pension plan to an RRSP. A number of restrictions apply, including withdrawal options and the types of retirement income that can be received. Regular and locked-in RRSPs are discussed in more detail in Chapter 8.

How Well Is Your Group RRSP Performing?

With most group RRSPs, employees have some degree of control over the investments made by the plan and therefore the performance of the plan. Under a group RRSP, the amount accumulated in the plan determines the size of the benefits that you will eventually collect. The types of retirement income which you can receive are dealt with in Chapter 8.

Group RRSPs have an advantage over individual plans in that volume contributing generally results in administrative savings and volume buying of investments can produce discounts on sales charges. The disadvantage is that often the group plan may be tied to one administrator, perhaps a mutual fund, trust company, bank or insurance company, which is inclined to acquire its own investment products and not shop the market for the best-performing funds or most advantageous investments. Dealing with one administrator that is locked into its own investment products makes life easy for the employer, but may not be in the best interests of the employees.

In the long run, it pays to know your plan. In the short run, before retirement, it is essential that you monitor both your plan's performance and your individual choice of investments. If your choice is limited and seems to be continually underperforming in terms of the market averages, you may want to try to convince your employer to deal with another administrator, or you might want to consider switching your accumulations in the group plan to a private plan that you control. This can be done on a tax-free basis as long as the funds are transferred directly to the new plan and are not received personally by you.

Can You Contribute More to Your Group RRSP?

If you are satisfied with the performance and advantages that your group RRSP offers, you might want to consider arranging for extra contributions, within your contribution limit, to be made to the plan. Possibly these will have to be made by your employer and be deducted directly from your paycheque. Check the contribution limit to see whether you have excess contribution room (see Chapter 8) and don't forget that you are allowed to make a cumulative over-contribution of up to $8,000.

One of the advantages of using your employer's group RRSP is that contributions are made directly by the employer on your behalf and the amount is deducted from your paycheque. In effect, you are receiving your tax deduction for the contribution immediately, rather than having to wait for a refund after filing your tax return, since your income tax withholdings on your paycheque are adjusted to accommodate the RRSP contribution.

RETIRING ALLOWANCES

A retiring allowance includes any amount received by an employee upon or after retirement in recognition of the services provided to his or her employer. Retiring allowances are taxable in full in the year they are received. However, it is easy to defer all or a portion of this tax on the retiring allowance by arranging for it to be transferred to your RRSP. The transfer cannot be made to your spouse's RRSP. If your employer makes the transfer directly, that is, you do not receive the funds, tax will not be withheld from your paycheque at the time the allowance is effectively paid to you.

Limits are placed on the amount of a retiring allowance that can be transferred on a tax-deferred basis to an RRSP. For each year of service with your employer, you are allowed to transfer up to $2,000 of the allowance to your RRSP. As well, for each year before 1989 that contributions to a pension plan or DPSP either were not made by your employer or, if made, did not vest to you, you may transfer an additional $1,500 of the retiring allowance to your RRSP. Note that the transfer does not have to be made to a locked-in RRSP.

If you receive the entire amount of your retiring allowance in one year and transfer the maximum to your RRSP, you may run into alternative minimum tax (AMT) problems. Even though the amount transferred to your RRSP can be deducted from income for tax purposes, this amount is not deductible when determining the amount of your income that is subject to the AMT. Before committing yourself to receiving the amount in one year, you should do a tax calculation before the end of the year to see if you will be affected by the AMT. If you will be liable for the AMT, you might want to arrange to receive a portion of the allowance in the year you retire and the remainder early in the immediately following year.

Chapter 6 — Other Company Deferrals

As you approach retirement age, one of your goals is to accumulate as much capital as possible so that, at some point, it will be able to generate retirement income. Depending on your position with your employer, a number of opportunities for increasing your wealth and augmenting your retirement resources may exist. You are probably already a member of a statutory plan, such as a registered pension plan or deferred profit sharing plan, and are maximizing your opportunities to save. However, there may be other methods for accumulation available from your employer. These can be divided into four broad categories:

- cash-based incentive plans;
- stock option plans;
- stock purchase plans;
- supplemental retirement arrangements.

The first three are most commonly used to reward senior employees and to provide a mechanism that promotes loyalty and longevity of employment. Many of these types of plans may be broadly based throughout the organization. Supplemental retirement arrangements almost always are the preserve of higher-level employees and are used to supplement their regular pension benefits. The maximum amounts that can be paid out of registered pension plans have lagged far behind salary increases over the last couple of decades, hence the popularity of these supplemental plans.

Before discussing the various arrangements that might be available to you, you should be aware that the Income Tax Act contains a variety of provisions that discourage and prevent almost all types of strategies attempting to defer the receipt and taxation of amounts that are earned by employees. Ideally, employers would prefer to incur the liability for the amount immediately and therefore receive the tax deduction when the liability is booked. However, the employer would also like to preserve current cash flow by delaying payment for some time, perhaps until the employee has retired and his or her tax rate has fallen.

Since employment income is generally taxed only when received, the employee would also like to delay receipt and postpone the date that tax becomes payable. Hopefully, the tax that will be payable in the future will be less than would be currently payable if the amount were to be received today. Of course, the employee also wants assurances that the amount will indeed be paid by the employer, even though he or she may be retired, and the employee wants to earn a reasonable rate of return on the amount until it is actually received.

Bear in mind that there is usually no point in delaying for a few years the receipt of an amount owed to you if you are not going to earn income on that amount during the deferral period. The tax saving that results from your tax rate declining by five or ten percentage points likely will prove to be a poor bargain. You would probably be much better off receiving the amount now, paying the tax, and starting to earn the investment income that the after-tax amount would generate. Deferring income ultimately comes down to making a financial decision. It may not be a tax strategy that is suitable for everybody.

CASH-BASED INCENTIVE PLANS

A variety of cash-based incentive plans are enjoyed by employees and can be used by them to shore up their retirement resources.

Year-End Bonuses

The most common cash-based incentive plan is the year-end bonus. You may be eligible for a cash bonus based on your performance during the year. Your performance may be measured against certain criteria, such as net income of your division for the year. Your employer receives a tax deduction in the year the bonus is declared, as long as it is actually paid within 180 days of the employer's fiscal year end. You do not have to report the bonus as income for tax purposes until the year you actually receive the cash. However, tax must be withheld from the bonus by the corporation when it is paid out.

Receiving your bonus in the calendar year you retire or the year after may result in a tax saving if your tax bracket has dropped a notch. In most provinces, there is a spread of about 6 to 9 percentage points between the top tax bracket and the middle bracket. The spread between the middle bracket and the lowest bracket is about 12 to 15 percentage points.

It is possible to delay receipt of your bonus. However, if it is not paid within 180 days of your employer's year end, your employer must reverse the deduction claimed in the year the bonus was declared and can claim it only in the year the bonus is actually paid. Because of the deductibility issue to the employer, most bonuses are paid within 180 days of the end of the employer's fiscal year.

Phantom Stock Plans

As the name implies, phantom stock plans do not involve the distribution of the company's stock, although the stock's value may come into play. Employees do not actually receive stock certificates under a phantom stock plan. Their incentive, which is paid in cash, may, in its simplest form, be based on the increase in the price of the employer corporation's stock. Or if that stock cannot be easily valued, some other valuation method for the worth of the employer will be employed. Phantom stock plans are particularly useful for remunerating senior employees of private corporations. Generally, the shareholders of such corporations are not anxious to introduce new shareholders, but they do want to encourage employees to participate in the growth of the company. Incentives tied to growth in the value of the enterprise are designed to accomplish this end.

One type of phantom stock plan provides that the employee becomes entitled to the cash value of either a real or a notional share of the employer corporation on the day the entitlement vests in the employee. A second, similar type of plan provides that the employee will receive a cash value equivalent to the increase in the value of the real or notional share between the day the employee begins to participate in the program and the vesting day. The first type is considered to fit within certain rules in the Income Tax Act pertaining to salary deferral arrangements. As a result, the value of the "share" must be included in the employee's income when he or she enters the program and tax is applied appropriately. The second type appears to avoid these rules and is the one commonly used by many employers.

STOCK OPTION ARRANGEMENTS

Stock options can prove to be a valuable source of additional resources for those getting close to retirement day. They have a number of advantages:

- There are no immediate tax consequences from being granted an option.
- When the option is exercised, the benefit may result in less tax than, for instance, additional salary or a bonus.
- When the optioned shares are sold, capital gains treatment applies and the gain is eligible for your $100,000 capital gains exemption.
- There is no downside to being entitled to stock options. If the stock declines in value, you simply decline to exercise the stock option.

Depending on the arrangement you have with your employer, stock options may or may not follow you into retirement. In some plans, you will be required to exercise those options available to you before you actually retire. And in almost all plans, you must still be an employee to be entitled to low-interest employee loans that may be available to enable you to acquire the stock when you choose to exercise your options. Such loans would have to be repaid upon retiring. Of course, you can sell some or all of the stock purchased with the loan and use the proceeds from the sale to repay the loan.

The amount of the taxable benefit arising on low- or no-interest loans from your employer is included in your income and is deductible for tax purposes as an interest expense if the proceeds are indeed used to exercise the option. If you borrow personally to finance the exercise of stock options, the interest paid is also deductible. In both cases, the interest will form part of your cumulative net investment loss (CNIL) for purposes of calculating your $100,000 capital gains exemption (see Chapter 10).

There are essentially two types of stock options — those that are issued by any corporation and those issued by a Canadian-controlled private corporation (CCPC). The tax treatment for each type differs considerably because of more favourable treatment accorded CCPCs.

For the first type of stock option, there are no income tax consequences when the option is granted to you, assuming that you have not paid any amount for the option. Upon exercise of the option, you are deemed to have received a benefit, which is fully taxable, equal to the difference between the option price and fair market value of the stock at the time the option is exercised. The full amount of the benefit is added to your cost of the shares. There are no capital gains consequences at this point. However, any future growth in the value of the stock will be considered a capital gain and on disposition would be eligible for your $100,000 capital gains exemption.

If you pay any amount for the option, it is simply added to the cost of the shares for purposes of determining any capital gain on disposition.

For example, assume that:

- the option price is $4;
- the fair market value (FMV) is $10 when you exercise the option;
- you sell the stock when it hits $14.

The stock option benefit of $6 ($10 minus $4) is included in your income for tax purposes in the year that you exercise the option. When the stock is sold for $14, your capital gain is $4. This gain may be eligible for your $100,000 capital gains exemption. Note that if you sell the option (not the shares), you will have taxable employment income equal to the amount of proceeds paid to you. Since this will be employment income, none of it will be eligible for the capital gains exemption.

If your stock option was granted after February 15, 1984, you may be entitled to a deduction in arriving at income for tax purposes when the option is exercised. The deduction is equal to one-quarter of the stock option benefit you included in your employment income. In the above example, your deduction would be $1.50 (1/4 of $6), which effectively reduces the taxable portion of your benefit to $4.50. Since only three-quarters of a capital gain is taxed, this is equivalent to getting capital gains treatment. However, note that you are not entitled to the $100,000 capital gains exemption. To qualify for the stock option deduction, you must deal at arm's length with the corporation and the exercise price of the stock must be equal to or greater than the fair market value of the stock at the time the option was granted, less any amounts paid for the option.

CCPC (Canadian-Controlled Private Corporation) Stock Options

The second type of stock option is referred to as a CCPC stock option. It receives more favourable tax treatment, but must meet the following conditions:

- The employer corporation must be a CCPC and the stock must be issued by that corporation or a CCPC that does not deal at arm's length with the employer corporation.
- You must be dealing at arm's length with the corporation immediately after exercising the option.
- You cannot dispose of your stock acquired pursuant to the option within two years (if you die, this rule is waived).

If these conditions are met, a stock option benefit equal to the difference between the option price and the fair market value of the stock at the time you exercised the option is included in your income in the year you actually sell the stock. As a result, the taxation of the stock option benefit is delayed until such time as you dispose of the shares. This also means that you should have the cash on hand to pay the tax. At the time the stock is sold, a tax deduction for one-quarter of the benefit is allowed, unless you sell the stock within two years of exercising the option. In the above example, the stock benefit would be $6 and be included in your income at the time you actually dispose of the stock. Your deduction, assuming that you hold the shares for more than two years, would be $1.50. The remaining $4 ($14 sale proceeds minus $10 FMV at the exercise date) is a capital gain eligible for your $100,000 exemption.

Note that the shares of a private corporation are not readily marketable. Thus, you might want to consider having a buy-sell agreement in place if you are participating in the plan. This would definitely be advisable as you approach retirement age, especially if the gains on your optioned shares are to form a part of your retirement fund. Such an agreement would generally guarantee that, on retirement or death, your shares would be purchased by the remaining shareholders. The purchase price may be set out in the agreement either as a specific amount or by formula, or may be simply left to be determined by a business valuator at the time of sale.

Stock options may appear attractive since there is virtually no downside for the employee — if the fair market value of the stock is higher than the option price, it is purchased; otherwise, the option is not exercised. However, a problem may crop up in certain situations. For example, if the condition imposed by the stock option agreement allows an affiliate of the company to buy back your shares for certain reasons, and they are sold at a loss, you will have a capital loss available. However, the stock benefit income inclusion was not considered a capital gain, so your loss can only be written off against gains that you realize on the sale of other capital properties. If you do not have any gains, either currently or in any of the preceding three years, the capital loss may have to be carried forward until such time that you do realize a capital gain. In other words, you will be taxed on the stock option benefit, but may never get any tax relief as a result of the loss you suffered on the sale of the shares.

STOCK PURCHASE PLANS

Stock purchase plans tend to be more broadly based among employees. Unlike stock option plans, stock purchase plans have a downside. If you are encouraged or required to buy stock in the company in lieu of receiving salary, and the stock declines in value, you are likely to look back on the arrangement as unsatisfactory and not look on the employer particularly kindly either.

In most situations, senior employees are provided with interest-free loans from the employer to enable them to purchase the company's stock. Such purchases can be quite large in some cases. If the plan is more broadly based, the employer may make cash contributions toward the purchase of the stock, and the amount that the employee can purchase may be based on salary and/or performance. These arrangements usually have some strings attached, since the employees are probably acquiring these shares at a substantial discount.

EMPLOYEE BENEFIT PLANS

Under an employee benefit plan, both the employee and the employer contribute to the plan and the plan buys the shares of the employer. At some time in the future, the vesting point, the employee becomes entitled to receive the shares from the plan. There is generally no taxable benefit to the employee at that time, if the shares are left in the plan. If the employee withdraws the shares, however, he or she will be in receipt of a taxable benefit equal to the difference between the fair market value of the shares at the time the shares vest in the employee and the amount that the employee contributed to the employee benefit plan. If the shares have gone up in value since they were purchased by the plan, the increase in value will not be a capital gain, but will be employment income. If the shares are left in the plan after vesting, future appreciation is considered to be a capital gain by Revenue Canada.

PRACTICAL POINTER   You will usually be required to withdraw your shares at retirement date, which could result in a significant amount of tax being paid in that year. As you near retirement, you might consider withdrawing shares periodically to spread the tax hit over several years.

The taxable benefit aspect is the major disadvantage of such plans, especially if the period to vesting is fairly lengthy. If the employer simply gave the employee the money that was contributed to the plan and the employee acquired the shares directly, any future appreciation would be a capital gain, only three-quarters of which is taxable, and may be eligible for the employee's $100,000 exemption.

EMPLOYEE PROFIT SHARING PLANS

Employee profit sharing plans (EPSPs) are more beneficial to employees because the employee is taxed only on amounts allocated to him or her. When the assets of the EPSP are distributed to the employee, there are no tax consequences at that time. As a result, these plans are similar to employee benefit plans, except that any contribution made by the employer is taxed in the hands of the employee as employment income for the year in which the contribution is received by the EPSP. As well, if the plan acquires shares with the employer's contributions, the employee is considered to have acquired these shares in the plan at their cost. Any dividends or gains realized by the plan flow through to the employee and are included in his or her income for tax purposes. However, when the shares vest in the employee or are distributed, there are no immediate tax consequences to the employee and no taxable benefit, because the employee has already been taxed in the year that the EPSP contributions were made. Capital gains will arise only when the shares are actually sold by the employee.

From the point of view of an employee approaching retirement age, EPSPs are far superior to employee benefit plans. You can wait until you retire to receive your shares from the plan, since there will be no further tax consequences. Or you can withdraw shares from the plan at any time, sell them, and use up your $100,000 capital gains exemption. You are also assured of getting your shares out of the plan, assuming that you meet the vesting requirements. The employer cannot withdraw contributions from the EPSP, whereas the employer might be able to take its contributions out of an employee benefit plan. This works to the employee's advantage in that, if some employees don't meet the vesting requirements, their amounts in the plan are distributed to the other members.

PRACTICAL POINTER   If you are a member of an EPSP and there is no danger of your not meeting all vesting requirements, consider leaving your investment in the plan for as long as possible. The longer you remain a member of the plan, the more likely it is that you will accumulate a portion of the shares of other members who have forfeited their investment because they have left the plan before meeting the vesting requirements.

UNTRUSTEED EMPLOYEE STOCK PURCHASE PLANS

These types of stock purchase plans are probably the most popular because they require the least administration by an employer. Generally, the employee designates a certain portion of his or her salary to be used to purchase the company's stock. The employer agrees to help with the purchase but this amount is simply added to the employee's salary. The stock is purchased in the employee's name. There is no vesting with this type of plan, but employers usually impose certain conditions, such as the employee must hold the shares for a certain period if the employer is to continue to help with future purchases.

If the shares are acquired from the company's treasury and are purchased at a discount, the difference between the purchase price and the current fair market value of the shares at the time of purchase is included in the employee's income as a taxable benefit. As you approach retirement age, these types of programs can be quite valuable since they augment your earnings. If you opt out of the program, you lose the benefit of the employer's contribution toward the stock purchase. Even though you are paying tax on this benefit, you are further ahead than if you purchased the stock yourself out of your after-tax funds.

The downside with these types of plans is that the value of the stock may decline during the period that you are expected to hold it in order to participate in future stock purchases with the employer's help. Upon retirement, this qualification obviously no longer applies, but this is just the time when you should be reviewing your investment portfolio and pruning it of the riskier investments. Your employer's shares may very well be one of those risky elements in your portfolio.

With any type of stock plan, you should be aware of the downside, as well as any protection offered. For example, if you are acquiring stock with interest-free employee loans and there is a program in place to forgive all or a portion of the loan should the value of the stock decline drastically, you may be more inclined to participate in the program than if that protection is not available (note that the forgiving of the loan would result in your receiving a taxable benefit). Or there may be an arrangement in place under which the employer is required to purchase the share from you if the price declines to a certain level. Or you may be given options to purchase preferred shares instead of common shares. These preferred shares would be convertible into common shares and may also be redeemable by the corporation. If the common shares decline in value, you would not exercise the conversion feature. If they increase in value, you would exercise the conversion option, receive the common shares, and then sell some or all of them.

SUPPLEMENTAL RETIREMENT ARRANGEMENTS

It is now virtually impossible to set up any kind of truly tax-advantaged retirement arrangement that also guarantees payments to the employee, other than those sanctioned by the Income Tax Act — registered pension plans, registered retirement saving plans, and deferred profit sharing plans. Every other type of arrangement will be caught by one anti-avoidance rule or another, unless the plan is relatively informal and contains no guarantees that benefits from the plan will actually be paid.

As might be expected, employers and employees are on opposite sides of the fence when it comes to preferring a particular kind of supplemental retirement arrangement. The employee wants early vesting of employer contributions to the plan and some sort of guarantee that the promised benefits will in fact be paid. After all, employees probably have little or no leverage once they retire, and they certainly can't control the fortunes of their former employer. If the employer's health declines, and the payments are not guaranteed, the employee may be out of luck. If arrangements are made when the employee is still some years away from retiring, the plan may have to make payments for 40 years or longer. The nature and health of a company can change dramatically over 40 years.

The employer, on the other hand, would prefer to have an informal, unfunded arrangement that pays the employee amounts out of current income once the employee retires. The tax consequences of setting up a guaranteed plan can be severe, while a plan that is not guaranteed is faced with no immediate tax problems.

Supplemental retirement arrangements come in a variety of shapes and sizes. The nature of particular plans depends to some extent on the bargaining power of the employees. Guaranteed funded plans that fall under the retirement compensation arrangement (RCA) rules are subject to specific tax laws. A plan that simply promises to pay current earnings in a later year will fall under the salary deferral arrangement (SDA) rules. The tax consequences here are even more adverse. Quite naturally, employers avoid such plans. Unfunded plans generally fall between the cracks, assuming that certain conditions are met.

RETIREMENT COMPENSATION ARRANGEMENTS OR FUNDED PLANS

A funded arrangement that guarantees payments will be made to the retiring employee is usually classified as an RCA. Under such a plan, contributions are made to a third-party trustee for the benefit of the employee, such benefits usually to be enjoyed upon retirement. Vesting of the contributions usually occurs quickly.

All contributions to an RCA are subject to a 50-per-cent tax when made and income earned in the RCA is subject to tax at the rate of 50 per cent. This tax is refundable as retirement benefits are received by the employee. Since the top corporate rate is considerably lower than 50 per cent, these plans are not very popular, except with very senior and quite valuable employees.

Note that such plans cannot serve simply to defer the employee's salary to a future year. If this is the case, they will be considered SDAs and more serious tax consequences will result.

LIFE INSURANCE OR ANNUITY ARRANGEMENTS

These are considered to be RCAs if the employer actually sets aside funds to buy the annuity or currently purchases insurance with a cash value. If the employer uses the annuity proceeds to pay the employee's retirement income, there is less security than if the employee is the beneficiary of the particular annuity or life insurance policy. In any case, if the company fails, creditors may have first call on the proceeds of either the annuity or the life insurance and, if so, the employee will be out of luck.

UNFUNDED SECURED PLANS

Simply promising the employee that supplemental retirement income will be paid at a certain rate for so many years is outside the ambit of both RCAs and SDAs. However, as explained above, employees would much prefer that these types of unfunded plans come with guarantees. In many cases, it may be possible for the employer to guarantee payment by a bank guarantee or letter of credit, security against assets of the employer, or perhaps a guarantee by another member of the corporate group. None of the methods is perfect, especially if the employer's fortunes decline drastically.

PRACTICAL POINTER   If you are expecting to leave Canada upon retiring, RCAs may be quite valuable, since there will only be a 25-per-cent withholding tax if you are receiving the funds while a non-resident. The 50-per-cent tax already paid is fully refundable, so your net tax will be 25 per cent. This tax should be creditable in many countries against tax paid in that jurisdiction.

EMPLOYER DEATH BENEFITS

Generally, up to $10,000 of a death benefit can be received by your spouse free of tax should you die while still employed. While not a large amount, a death benefit should form part of your remuneration package during your pre-retirement years, if possible.

Chapter 7 — Retirement Benefits from Your Employer

Most employees enjoy a variety of fringe benefits while they are employed, ranging from company cars or interest-free loans, to discounts on the employer's merchandise and free extended health care. Not all these benefits will continue to be available once you retire, but some might follow you into retirement as a matter of course, since they are part of the standard retirement benefit package. And you may be able to negotiate for others to be available.

Many fringe benefits are caught by the taxable benefit rules in the tax law, but a number are specifically exempted, or have special rules which apply. Generally, the value of a benefit caught by the rules is added to your employment income. Value for these purposes is usually fair market value, not the cost to the employer. Furthermore, the tax rules provide that, in order for a benefit to exist, it must be received or enjoyed in respect of, in the course of, or by virtue of employment. This last phrase "by virtue of employment" is very broad and can apply to individuals who have retired. To be subject to the taxable benefit rules, there simply has to have been an employee–employer relationship at some time.

Having a benefit included in your employment income for tax purposes isn't the disaster you might think. If the benefit is something on which you would normally have spent your after-tax dollars, you are much better off incurring the taxable benefit than paying for the good or service out of your own pocket. For example, let's say that your employer lets you use the company yacht for a week free of charge in the year after you retire. Assume that renting such a boat for a week would normally set you back $2,000. The value of the week's free use of the yacht ($2,000) is added to your income, which you report in your tax return for that year. Assuming that your marginal rate of tax is 40 per cent, you will pay $800 tax (40 per cent of $2,000) on this benefit. Obviously, you are much better off paying the tax of $800 than forking out $2,000 of your retirement income for the use of the boat for a week.

COUNSELLING SERVICES

Generally, counselling services paid for or provided by the employer will be taxable. However, employment counselling services, usually associated with terminated employees, and retirement counselling are not taxable. The service may be provided directly by the employer, or supplied by an outside agency and paid for by the employer. If you pay for the retirement or employment counselling yourself and are reimbursed by your employer, the reimbursement will be taxable.

Note that financial counselling services are taxable. Drawing the line between retirement and financial counselling will not always be easy. Generally, Revenue Canada views financial counselling as a recurring service with no particular emphasis on retirement. Retirement counselling is usually non-recurring and takes place at or near (within 15 years of) retiring. Any advice that relates to the purchase of specific investments or promotes a specific investment strategy does not qualify as retirement counselling.

LOW- OR NO-INTEREST LOANS

In most situations, you will be required to repay any loans you have received from your employer at the time you retire. Often such loans are received to finance the purchase of the employer corporation's stock, or to enable the employee to acquire a home. If your negotiating position is particularly strong during your last few years of work, you may be able to arrange for repayment of the loan during retirement, not at the time you retire.

Unless interest is charged on the loan at market rates or at the prescribed rate set by the government, a taxable benefit will result. The benefit is measured as the difference between interest that would be payable on the outstanding balance of the loan at the prescribed rate and any interest actually paid by the employee during the year or within 30 days after the end of the year. A loan will be deemed to have been made if you purchase assets from your employer, and an outstanding balance of the purchase price remains to be paid at the end of the year.

Three points should be noted. First, if the funds borrowed from the employer are used to acquire income-producing assets, you are entitled to deduct for tax purposes an amount equal to the taxable benefit included in your income. Second, if your loan is forgiven by your employer, the amount forgiven is included in your income for tax purposes in that year. Third, special rules apply to certain housing loans. For loans that enable you to purchase a home or refinance your mortgage, the prescribed rate at the time you make the loan stays in effect for five years. For home relocation loans, any taxable benefit is reduced by the benefit that would otherwise apply to an interest-free loan of $25,000.

All these rules apply even though you are retired.

PRACTICAL POINTER   **If your employer plans to forgive an out-standing loan once you are retired, you should try to arrange to have it forgiven over a period of years if you are not in the top tax bracket. This should prevent at least a portion of the taxable benefit being taxed at the top rate.**

STOCK OPTIONS

Stock options were discussed in detail in the previous chapter. The same treatment applies, even though options are exercised either at the time you retire or some time after you retire. It is highly unlikely that you will be able to obtain a loan from your former employer to finance the exercise of an option, since any borrowing by your employer for such a purpose would likely not be deductible, as you are no longer an employee.

ACCESS TO COMPANY ASSETS

Many retired employees continue to enjoy access to company assets, such as the company condo down south or in a ski area, a summer cottage, or perhaps a yacht or airplane. Generally, any use by you will result in a taxable benefit. Determining the value of the benefit is another matter. Revenue Canada generally looks at fair market value rent as the appropriate value. You would much prefer the employer's cost to be used as the value of the benefit.

Very specific rules apply if you continue to use an automobile owned by your ex-employer. These are somewhat complicated and are discussed thoroughly in the Deloitte & Touche book *How to Reduce the Tax You Pay.*

Some employers continue to make temporary office space, meeting rooms, and secretarial services available to retired employees who may be operating their own businesses. This should usually result in a taxable benefit. Valuing the benefit could be difficult. From the employer's point of view, these amenities would be available whether or not they were used by a retired employee, and therefore their incremental cost is negligible. On the other hand, such facilities are often available on a monthly rental basis, and this might be the figure Revenue Canada uses to determine the taxable benefit. There is generally no benefit attached to such services if an employee is terminated and uses them to search for another job. Whether this would be the case with an employee who retires but uses the facilities to seek a part-time consulting position is questionable.

RECREATIONAL FACILITIES

More and more employers are providing their employees with various recreational facilities on site. There is usually no taxable benefit associated with an employee's use of such facilities as long as they are available to all employees on an equitable basis. If you continue to use the facilities once you retire, there should be no taxable benefit.

There is generally no taxable benefit if your employer pays your fees at a recreational or social club if the reason for your membership is principally for your employer's advantage and not yours. In other words, such clubs generally must be used for meeting and entertaining clients or associates and there must be a business purpose behind most such encounters. If you retire and your ex-employer continues to pay your club dues, you will likely be assessed a taxable benefit, unless you continue to use the club primarily for your employer's business advantage. If you continue to provide services for your ex-employer's benefit, you might consider attaching a value to them and acting as a consultant to your ex-employer.

DISCOUNTS ON EMPLOYER MERCHANDISE OR SERVICES

There is no taxable benefit if an employer's goods or services are sold to employees for not less than the employer's cost. If these goods or services are given away or sold for less than cost, an appropriate taxable benefit will apply. Note that the goods or services must be those supplied by the employer. Goods supplied at cost by another company, even though it might be related to the employer, will result in a taxable benefit. These rules continue to apply to retired employees. If there is an outstanding amount on the purchase price of the goods or services, there may be an imputed taxable benefit, as explained earlier for low- or no-interest loans.

ACQUISITION OF EMPLOYER-OWNED ASSETS ON RETIREMENT

If an employee acquires an asset, such as an automobile or computer, owned by the employer, a benefit will usually result unless fair market value is paid for the asset. This is the case even though the employee may have taken less salary near his or her retirement date and acquired the asset for a substantial discount.

Similarly, if you have been using company assets and they are not returned to your employer at retirement, a benefit could result. On the other hand, if your employer financed a security system for your home, because you often worked on sensitive documents at home over the weekend, it may be more difficult to determine a benefit, if any, that must be included in your income. In most such cases, a benefit was likely included in your income at the time the asset was acquired, so no further taxable benefit will likely result.

HEALTH CARE

Premiums paid by your employer for health care under a provincial health insurance plan produce a taxable benefit. This would continue to be the case if your ex-employer carried on paying these premiums after you retired.

However, benefits provided to employees or ex-employees under a private health care plan do not constitute a taxable benefit. Such plans usually provide for extended coverage that is either in excess of provincial coverage or not covered under the provincial plan, such as dental care.

MOVING EXPENSES

If you relocate on or after retirement and your ex-employer pays your moving expenses, you will be in receipt of a taxable benefit. Still, as explained earlier, you are much better off paying the tax on the benefit than paying for the moving expenses out of your own pocket. Neither the amount included in income as a taxable benefit nor the tax that you actually pay would be eligible to be deducted for tax purposes as a moving expense deduction.

If you relocate while still employed, there is no taxable benefit associated with moving costs and certain other costs borne by your employer. For example, if you are reimbursed for a loss suffered on the sale of your home on a relocation required by your employer, there is no taxable benefit. As well, there is no benefit if the employer guarantees to give you a sum equal to the amount by which the fair market value of the home exceeds the actual selling price. And no benefit arises if your employer purchases your home, as long as the purchase price does not exceed fair market value. As can be appreciated, you could be much better off relocating before you retire rather than waiting until after your retirement date, if such an arrangement can be worked out with your employer.

LIFE INSURANCE

There is no taxable benefit if you are covered under a group life insurance plan with your employer and coverage does not exceed $25,000. If coverage exceeds this threshold, only the premium relating to the excess coverage produces a taxable benefit. In virtually all situations, your coverage under the group policy would lapse once you retired.

If your employer has taken out a policy on you specifically, a benefit will arise if the policy is transferred over to you at less than fair market value.

TUITION FEES

Generally, tuition fees paid for, or on behalf of, an employee by the employer must be reported as a taxable benefit. However, if the employee registers for the course on the employer's initiative and for the benefit of the employer, there is no taxable benefit if the employer pays for the tuition. This would not be the case for courses that you take after you retire and which are paid for by your ex-employer. Note that any non-taxable benefit would not be eligible for the tuition fee tax credit.

Chapter 8 — Getting Your RRSPs in Shape

If you are not using RRSPs (registered retirement savings plans) to save for your retirement, you should be. The advantages of this great Canadian tax shelter cannot be overstated.

- Contributions within prescribed limits are fully tax-deductible.
- All income earned inside the RRSP is tax-sheltered.
- Amounts in RRSPs become taxable only when you actually receive them.
- You do not have to arrange to begin receiving amounts in your RRSP until after the year you turn age 71.
- Depending on how you arrange to receive your RRSP funds, a portion could remain tax-sheltered well into your nineties.
- You can contribute to your spouse's RRSP within limits. He or she can then receive and be taxed on the amounts upon retirement, which should reduce the tax bill for the family as a whole.
- You have control over how much of your RRSP forms part of your estate on death, which is generally not possible with conventional registered pension plans.

The RRSP contribution rules became considerably more complex several years ago with the introduction of pension tax reform. Limits on your contributions are now tightly integrated with how much is contributed to other retirement plans, as well as the size of the benefit earned in the year from certain of those plans. Fortunately, in the tax assessment that you usually receive a few weeks after filing your tax return, the government reports how much you are eligible to contribute to an RRSP in respect of the current year. Further changes in your contribution room may be reported to you later in the year. For those who are not members of RPPs or DPSPs, the amount will also be found on the notice of assessment that you receive a few weeks after filing your annual tax return.

CONTRIBUTION LIMITS

How much you can contribute each year depends on your earned income, which is essentially salary or wages, business income, net rental income, taxable alimony or maintenance payments, royalties, income from supplementary unemployment benefit plans, and net research grants. Losses from businesses and rental properties, as well as deductible alimony and maintenance payments, reduce your earned income.

If you are not a member of an RPP or DPSP, your contribution limit is 18 per cent of your prior year's earned income to a maximum dollar limit. In the February 1992 budget, the government proposed to adjust the maximum dollar limits as follows:

1993 $12,500
1994 $13,500
1995 $14,500
1996 $15,500

In 1993, you need earned income of at least $69,444 to make the maximum contribution of $12,500. After 1996, the upper limit is indexed according to increases in the average wage figures that are used to determine contribution limits for the C/QPP.

THE PENSION ADJUSTMENT

If you belong to a DPSP or an RPP, your contribution limit to an RRSP is reduced by the amount of your prior year's pension adjustment, or PA. The PA for a DPSP or a defined contribution RPP is the actual amount contributed to those plans in a particular year by both you and your employer (note that employees can no longer contribute to DPSPs).

If you belong to a defined benefit RPP, the pension adjustment is based on the benefits you accumulate in the prior year in the RPP. Generally, if you belong to a generous RPP, your PA will be quite large, which in turn restricts how much you can contribute to your RRSP in the following year. If your plan is not so generous, your PA will be smaller, which results in higher allowable RRSP contributions. No matter what the size of your PA, you are allowed to contribute at least $1,000 to your RRSP each year.

Employers must calculate an employee's PA each year and report it on the employee's T4 slip, which is usually received in late February following the year to which the PA relates. This should permit you to calculate your allowable RRSP contribution relatively early in the year because you compute your allowable RRSP contribution using both your earned income and your PA of the previous calendar year. Revenue Canada also reports this limit to you later in the year.

If you or your employer make past service contributions to your RPP to enhance post-1989 benefits, your RRSP contribution limit may be reduced. This may occur, for example, if the benefits of your RPP are upgraded or if you "purchase" additional years of service.

CONTRIBUTION ROOM CARRY-FORWARDS

If you contribute less than the maximum to your RRSP in any particular year, you are permitted to make up for this unused contribution room in any of the succeeding seven years by contributing more than the maximum for that future year. Contributions in a succeeding year are first applied to contribution room remaining from a prior year and then to contribution room for the current year. Generally, there will be no tax saving in purposely delaying an RRSP contribution if you expect your tax rate to increase in a succeeding year. In fact there could be a tax cost. As well, delaying your contribution will result in smaller accumulations in your RRSP because the funds are invested for a shorter period of time.

That's why it may pay to borrow for your RRSP contribution, even though the interest expense on the loan is not deductible for tax purposes. Delaying the contribution for a year or two may save you the interest expense, but the benefits gained from sheltering the investment income from tax in the RRSP and gaining the tax deduction for the contribution could outweigh any savings. Also, most institutions are currently offering extremely attractive interest rates if the borrowed funds are contributed to an RRSP at that institution.

PRACTICAL POINTER   If you contribute to your RRSP in any particular year, you might consider not claiming the deduction in that year, but claiming it in the following year, assuming that you have sufficient contribution room available. This would only make sense if you knew that your tax rate would rise in the following year and the contribution would be deductible against income taxed at the higher rate in that year, resulting in a larger tax saving.

As noted at the beginning of the chapter, you may contribute to your spouse's RRSP within your annual limits. Spousal RRSPs are discussed in more detail in Chapter 10.

For a contribution to be deductible in a particular year, it must be made to your RRSP, or your spouse's RRSP for a spousal contribution, at any time after 1990 or within the first 60 days of the immediately following year and it must not have been previously deducted.

CONTRIBUTIONS IN KIND

You may contribute either cash or qualifying investments to your RRSP. Generally, investments may be contributed only to self-directed RRSPs, which are discussed later in this chapter. When you contribute a non-cash item to your RRSP, for example, shares in a public company, you are deemed to have disposed of the investment for its fair market value at the time it is transferred to the RRSP. Any gain must be recognized for tax purposes, and may be eligible for your lifetime capital gains exemption. Losses from a sale to your RRSP are denied for tax purposes. Thus, there is no point in selling a loser to your RRSP.

PRACTICAL POINTER   If you have a self-directed RRSP and generally buy securities on which sizeable brokerage commissions are charged, you may be better off buying them outside the RRSP and transferring

them into the plan as part of your annual contribution. If you contribute cash, the commissions incurred on a subsequent purchase are deducted within your RRSP, which results in smaller accumulations. If you make the purchase outside the plan, you are allowed to contribute the full value of the security to your RRSP. The commission paid personally is used to increase the cost base of your security. So if you make the transfer to your RRSP immediately after buying the security, you may incur a loss which cannot be recognized for tax purposes. You should try to wait until the security has increased in value sufficiently to offset the commission paid on its purchase before transferring it your RRSP. Generally, there is no charge for transferring a security owned personally to your RRSP.

Note that none of your RRSP contributions are allowed as a deduction in arriving at the amount of your income that is subject to the alternative minimum tax (AMT). As mentioned in Chapter 5, the AMT is an alternative calculation of income taxes. It was the federal government's response to concerns that some high-income individuals were taking advantage of tax incentives and sheltering virtually all of their income from tax. The calculation of the AMT involves the denial of certain deductions normally claimed for "regular" tax purposes. RRSP contributions are one of the deductions denied under the AMT rules.

The AMT will generally not affect you if you have no other non-deductible income items and your RRSP contribution simply reflects your annual limit. However, if you are making large catch-up contributions or transferring large amounts to your RRSP as a result of receiving a retiring allowance, you could have an AMT problem. You may be better off delaying a portion of your large RRSP contribution to the succeeding year. However, bear in mind that the excess of your AMT liability over your regular tax bill is deductible in any of the next seven years, but only to the extent that your regular tax liability exceeds your AMT liability in that year. Thus, you generally have the ability to recover some or all of the AMT you may have paid in prior years.

OVERCONTRIBUTING

You are allowed to "overcontribute" up to $8,000 to your RRSP. This is a cumulative limit. Once you reach the $8,000 limit, you may not make any overcontributions without penalty unless you reduce the overcontribution outstanding. This is done by designating the overcontribution amount as a regular contribution in a succeeding year. If you exceed the limit, the penalty is a tax of 1 per cent a month of the excess amount for each month it remains in the plan. However, you are permitted to remove the excess amount tax-free in the year you receive a notice of assessment specifically mentioning the excess amount or in the following year. If you leave the excess amount in your plan, you will, in effect, be subject to double taxation, since you will be denied a deduction for the contribution and will be taxed when the funds are eventually withdrawn.

PRACTICAL POINTER   Maintaining an $8,000 overcontribution in your RRSP makes good tax sense. You don't receive a tax deduction for the contribution but the income earned on the $8,000 accumulates tax-free. This would not be possible if you invested the $8,000 outside your RRSP. Generally, the $8,000 overcontribution should be earmarked for securities on which the income would normally be taxed heavily in your hands, such as interest-bearing investments.

Your RRSP could be subject to a variety of other taxes and penalties if you break the RRSP rules. These will be assessed, for example, if your RRSP acquires a non-qualifying investment, arranges to borrow money, invests directly in real estate, or exceeds the foreign investment content limit. In 1993, your RRSP is permitted to hold up to 18 per cent of the cost of its total investments in qualifying foreign securities. This limit tops out at 20 per cent in 1994 and subsequent years. This limit may be exceeded if you invest in certain eligible small businesses.

TRANSFERS TO AND FROM YOUR RRSP

If you are in receipt of periodic payments from an RPP or a DPSP, up to $6,000 can be transferred to a spousal RRSP in each of 1993 and 1994. The transfer must be made within 60 days of the end of the year to qualify. Otherwise, you are not allowed to transfer any periodic pension benefit to a tax-sheltered RRSP.

Amounts in your RRSP can be transferred directly by the issuer on a tax-free basis to another RRSP, to an RRIF, or to an RPP.

PRACTICAL POINTER   You might consider transferring an amount from your RRSP to your defined benefit RPP if, for example, your plan has been upgraded and your employer will finance half the cost of the upgrades. Of course, you should compare the benefits of receiving the upgrades or leaving the funds in your RRSP to accumulate until you require them.

You are allowed to make direct transfers of certain amounts from an RRIF to an RRSP or to another RRIF. As well, a "refund of premiums", which is received by your spouse or certain other dependants from your RRSP upon your death, can be transferred on a tax-free basis to the person's RRSP. Furthermore, the tax-free transfer of RRSP amounts between spouses or former spouses is permitted on the breakdown of a marriage.

LOCKED-IN RRSPs

Locked-in RRSPs must generally be used when accumulated pension benefits from an RPP are transferred to an RRSP. These benefits cannot be transferred to a regular RRSP. As the name implies, the rules for locked-in RRSPs are much more restrictive than for a regular RRSP. In most provinces, the funds are locked in until retirement age, usually age 60 or later, and the only type of retirement income you can receive is a life annuity. However, Quebec has pioneered the use of Life Income Funds (LIFs) as a way of receiving funds from a locked-in RRSP. Ontario agreed to join the LIF bandwagon late in 1992, and Alberta, Saskatchewan, Manitoba, and Nova Scotia are also committed. Generally, funds from the locked-in RRSP are transferred to the LIF. You can manage the investment of these funds much the same way that you do with an RRSP. Withdrawals are allowed within certain limits (there are minimums and maximums), although an annuity must be purchased with the remaining funds when you turn 80. In Ontario, the consent of your spouse or common-law spouse will be required before the purchase of an LIF, and your spouse or common-law spouse will have to be the sole beneficiary of the LIF.

PRACTICAL POINTER   More and more workers are accumulating funds in locked-in RRSPs as it becomes more common to move from job

to job. LIFs are an option everyone should consider, especially now that annuity rates have plummeted with low-interest rates. An LIF gives you the option of biding your time with your RRSP funds until interest rates reach more attractive levels. If you have no desire to buy an annuity until you reach 80, LIFs provide the flexibility of managing your own retirement funds just as you managed your RRSPs.

TYPES OF RRSPs

There are three major categories of RRSPs:

- insurance type, under which you contract to contribute a certain amount over a period of time, in return for a retirement income of a certain size paid periodically (an annuity);
- depositary type, under which your contributions are made directly with the issuer and the particular investment purchased is registered as an RRSP;
- RRSP trust, the most common of which are self-directed RRSPs where you make the investment decisions.

Insurance companies can issue only the first type of RRSP, since the retirement income is structured as a life annuity. The second type is offered by all financial institutions and comes in a wide variety of forms. Most self-directed plans are offered by securities brokers and trust companies.

Once your RRSP holdings reach a certain size, it may pay to begin using a self-directed RRSP, which generally provides convenient monthly reporting from one source and facilitates the spreading and varying of risk. As your investment objectives change over time, the make-up of a self-directed portfolio can be updated, which provides maximum flexibility.

PRACTICAL POINTER   An annual RRSP administration fee may be charged by a number of your RRSPs, usually mutual-fund types of plans. If you have several such plans, these fees could amount to several hundred dollars each year. With a self-directed plan, you pay only one administration fee. If this fee is paid personally outside the plan, it is deductible for tax purposes. As well, you will not be depleting funds inside your RRSP, which should allow for larger accumulations.

INVESTING IN YOUR RRSP

Conventional wisdom has it that you should be investing more cautiously and more conservatively the closer you are to retirement age. You have less time to make up for mistakes that you might make and you want to preserve the capital that you have managed to accumulate over the years. The second point is certainly true. You have spent the last 20 or 30 years working and saving so that you can enjoy a comfortable retirement. To put that at risk at this stage of the game makes no sense at all.

The first point doesn't always hold up well under closer scrutiny. It all depends on when you plan to use your RRSP funds during your retirement years. If you are 60 and within a couple of years of retiring, but won't be maturing your RRSPs until age 71, your investment horizon is at least 11 years, which in anybody's books could be considered long-term. If you transfer your RRSPs into an RRIF (see below) and take the minimum payments from the RRIF, a large portion of your tax-sheltered funds could remain intact for 15 or 20 years and even longer.

Thus, there may be little point in rushing out to convert many of your longer-term, riskier equity investments into shorter-term, less risky interest-bearing investments. If you are satisfied that your capital is not at serious risk, and you feel that you can bear the risk for some time to come, there may be little harm in continuing to think of long-term equity investing. Of course, you may want to turn your mind to less speculative securities.

However, if you plan to convert your RRSPs into retirement income within a few years and will be heavily dependent on that income, you could be better off converting your equity investments into interest-bearing ones so that you can begin to get a handle on how much you can realistically expect to accumulate from your RRSPs. This will allow you to better estimate the size of the retirement income that your RRSP will generate and consequently better plan your finances once you retire.

This is also the time to ensure that you are making the maximum use of your $100,000 lifetime capital gains exemption. This is available to all residents of Canada and it allows you to realize capital gains on most investments free of tax, up to the cumulative lifetime maximum of $100,000 (taxable portion of $75,000). There is actually no difference between realizing capital gains inside your RRSP and doing so outside it. Both are essentially tax-free, assuming that you have your lifetime exemption available. However, if you are earning interest income outside your RRSP and capital gains inside, you would definitely be better off shifting your investments around so that tax-free gains are earned outside your RRSP and the interest is sheltered from tax inside your plan. Remember that interest is taxed at your marginal rate when you earn it personally.

With the failure of a number of trust companies over the last decade or so, security of capital has assumed much greater importance to RRSP investors. If you have RRSP deposits at a chartered bank, a federally incorporated trust company, or a mortgage loan company, your investment will generally be covered by the CDIC (Canada Deposit Insurance Corporation). Provincially chartered trust and mortgage loan companies may also apply for membership with the CDIC.

The CDIC does not cover foreign currency deposits, foreign currency GICs (guaranteed investment certificates), or any type of mutual fund offered by these institutions. As well, the coverage is limited to only $60,000 per institution. As you get closer to retirement, your RRSP accumulations will likely be much greater than $60,000, so it may pay to spread your depositary-type RRSPs around among different issuers.

The insurance industry, credit unions, the mutual funds industry, and the brokerage industry maintain some type of coverage to protect investors in the event that any of their members gets into financial difficulty. You should ascertain exactly how extensive this coverage is and what kind of guarantees are provided to you by the relevant institution.

MAXIMIZING YOUR RRSP ACCUMULATIONS

The closer you get to retiring, the more concerned you are likely to become that your RRSP just isn't growing fast enough to meet your income expectations. There are no sure-fire ways to ensure that your RRSP investment portfolio earns 25 per cent rather than 10 per cent. Accepting more risk may increase the annual rate of return, but then again it may not. Accepting more risk may also lead to an actual erosion of your capital in some years, perhaps the very years that you plan to turn your RRSP into retirement income, so that you actually end up having a smaller amount of RRSP retirement income than you originally expected.

Nevertheless, there are a couple of things you can do to ensure that you are giving your RRSP every chance to generate the best possible retirement income.

PRACTICAL POINTERS

- It will always pay to contribute to your RRSP as early in the year as possible. The sooner the funds get into your plan, the sooner they begin earning tax-sheltered investment income. In fact, if you contribute at the beginning of the year instead of at the end of the year, each and every year you have an RRSP, you will end up with an extra year's investment earnings in your plan when you retire. If the plan is earning 10 per cent in the year you retire, that's 10 per cent more that is available to convert into a retirement income.
- We mentioned earlier that you should try to make the maximum $8,000 overcontribution as soon as you can. The investment income earned is tax-sheltered, and you will be able to claim a regular deduction for the $8,000 in the year after you retire, assuming that you have $8,000 of normal contribution room in that year.
- Make sure you contribute to a spousal RRSP. If you expect your spouse to be in a lower tax bracket than you at retirement, spousal contributions make a great deal of sense. Your spouse will receive the RRSP retirement income and be taxed on it. If his or her marginal tax rate is 27 per cent and yours is 50 per cent, that's a saving of 23 cents on every RRSP retirement dollar that the two of you receive. Spousal RRSPs are discussed in more detail in Chapter 10.
- It goes without saying that you and your spouse should maximize your contributions each and every year. Many people get in the habit of contributing a fixed dollar amount to their plans each year rather than a percentage of their income or the maximum that they are allowed under the RRSP rules. Revenue Canada supplies a booklet in which you can calculate your maximum allowable contribution (the *Pension and RRSP Tax Guide* — available from your district taxation office).
- Review your investments periodically. A monthly review is ideal but you should go over your RRSP portfolio at least twice a year. Too many Canadians buy their RRSPs in February, put them in a drawer and forget about them until the issuer lets them know their investment has matured and must be reinvested. If the contribution was put into a savings account type of RRSP, it's possible to just forget about it until age

71. Savings accounts currently are earning only a fraction of what they were a couple of years ago. This is no way to ensure that your RRSP funds begin to mount up significantly.

If you still have a mortgage as you approach retirement age, it won't be easy deciding between contributing the maximum to your RRSP and paying down your mortgage with these extra funds. At this point, you should ideally be doing both so that your mortgage is discharged before the day you retire and your RRSP accumulations have been maximized. If it looks like your mortgage may still be hanging around come retirement day, you probably will be better off diverting your potential RRSP contributions into the pay down of your mortgage. Chances are that any new investments you would make in your RRSP with the contribution would go into relatively conservative interest-bearing securities. And chances are that these would be earning less than the rate of interest that you are paying on your mortgage. Generally, you are better off paying down your mortgage if the rate of interest is higher than the earnings rate in your RRSP. As you near retirement age, the spread between the rates would have to be several percentage points in favour of the RRSP before it would be better to maximize your RRSP contributions and go into retirement with a mortgage.

CONVERTING YOUR RRSP INTO RETIREMENT INCOME

By December 31 of the year you turn age 71, you must convert your RRSPs into a "retirement income", that is, they must be matured. If you fail to choose one of the retirement income options, the entire amount in your RRSPs will be included in your income in the following year and be subject to tax. Chances are good that it will be taxed at the top marginal tax rate in your province (perhaps 50 per cent or even higher) and you will have no opportunity to defer this tax. Once you have matured your RRSPs, you must begin receiving retirement income by the end of the immediately following year.

With insurance-type RRSPs, maturing the plan simply means that you begin to receive the RRSP retirement income stipulated in the plan. With the other types of RRSPs, there are essentially two retirement income options. You can choose either to convert your

RRSP funds into an annuity and begin receiving the annuity payments, or to transfer your RRSP funds into a registered retirement income fund (RRIF) and begin receiving payments out of the RRIF. Of course you also have the option of collapsing your RRSPs at any time and receiving a lump-sum after paying the relevant taxes.

Bear in mind that you can shop around for annuities and RRIFs. They do not have to be purchased from the issuer of your RRSP. Rates and terms vary, depending on the issuer of the retirement income. You might want to consider using an annuities broker or other retirement professional to shop the market and determine the best rates and terms for the types of RRSP retirement income that you desire.

You can choose any combination of the retirement options. You can have any number of several different types of annuities and have more than one RRIF. Of course you may also elect to collapse a portion of your RRSP holdings and receive cash upon retiring. This degree of flexibility can be extremely valuable. For example, you may want a quick infusion of cash once you retire to finance large expenditures, such as extensive travel or the purchase of a second home. You also may want to acquire a life annuity to assure a steady stream of income should you live to a ripe old age. And you may want to use a RRIF or an indexed annuity to assure that your retirement income contains a fair degree of inflation protection.

This flexibility does not stop once you have decided on your retirement income options. Funds can be switched from one RRIF to another if you are unhappy with its performance or options. You can withdraw any amount from your RRIF at any time, as long as a specified minimum amount is withdrawn each year. You can convert amounts in RRIFs to life annuities at any time you choose. Depending on the term of the particular annuity, you may be able to commute it and receive the cash, after paying the appropriate tax, of course. However, amounts withdrawn from a RRIF in excess of the required minimum and any commuted annuity amounts may be transferred directly on a tax-deferred basis to another RRIF, or even to an RRSP if you are under age 72. Finally, you may be able to acquire an impaired health annuity from some life insurance companies if you can establish that your life expectancy is considerably shorter than the statistical norm. These types of annuities provide for larger payments, although you may be able to accomplish the same result with a RRIF by taking out large initial payments from the plan when it is first established.

Maturing your RRSPs before it is absolutely necessary means that you give up a portion of the tax-sheltering effects of the RRSP, and it may also result in a smaller retirement income because there is less in your RRSP to generate that income.

PRACTICAL POINTER   Consider maturing only a portion or, if you have several RRSPs, only some of your plans to generate only the income that you will need upon retiring. However, if you are age 65 and have no other source of *pension* income, definitely consider maturing a sufficient portion of your RRSPs to produce at least $1,000 of RRSP retirement income a year so that you maximize the pension income tax credit, which is worth about $270 in tax savings, depending on your province of residence.

In one particular situation, you might consider maturing your RRSP before you actually need the funds. This could occur if you are planning on buying an annuity, interest rates are particularly high at the current time, and you expect interest rates to drop substantially by the time you would normally expect to acquire the annuity with your RRSP funds. Of course, you are making an investment decision that entails a considerable amount of risk. If rates do not decline, you will be receiving income that you can't necessarily use, and paying tax on it. If rates decline only moderately, the advantage that you gain from receiving a larger income from the annuity because of the higher rates may not outweigh the benefits that you would have derived by not giving up the tax shelter of the RRSP. Of course, assuming that you have sufficient earned income and you have not reached age 71, you can continue to contribute to your other RRSPs, even though you have begun to receive RRSP annuity income.

RRSP ANNUITIES

There are two basic types of annuities that can be acquired with RRSP funds — life annuities and fixed-term or term-certain annuities. Each type can come with a variety of bells and whistles.

A life annuity guarantees to pay the annuitant an income for life. Payments must be made periodically and no less frequently than once a year. The first payment must be made in the year following the year you purchase the annuity. The size of the payments that you receive depends primarily on your age, that is, your life expectancy, and on current interest rates. The longer you can be expected to live, the smaller the payments from the annuity will be. High interest rates will result in larger annuity payments than if interest rates are low.

Fixed-term RRSP annuities are payable from the time you acquire the annuity to the year you turn age 90. If your spouse is younger than you, you may base the term on your spouse's age.

With a basic life annuity, the payments stop once the annuitant dies. The payments from a fixed-term annuity, or the commuted value of the annuity, are payable to the annuitant's heirs on the annuitant's death, or the annuitant's spouse may opt to step into the annuitant's shoes and continue to receive the payments.

Guarantee terms can be added to life annuities. These are typically for ten or fifteen years, which means payments (or the equivalent commuted value) become available on the death of the annuitant. As well, you can opt to buy a joint and last survivor life annuity, which means that payments continue to your surviving spouse upon your death. These payments continue to be made until your spouse dies. Both the guarantee option and the joint survivor option reduce the amount of your annuity payments, all other things being equal.

Both of the basic types of annuities can be indexed. Life annuities may be indexed to actual increases in the cost of living, as measured by the government's Consumer Price Index. As well, several life insurance companies offer annuities that are indexed according to increases in value in a pool of interest-bearing securities. Both these types of annuities will produce variable increases each year and so may not be suitable to retirees who want a steady and predictable stream of retirement income.

You should note that payments in the early years from indexed annuities are much lower than those received from annuities that are not indexed. For example, if you retire at age 65 and choose a fixed-term annuity indexed at 4 per cent annually, your initial payment will be about 70 per cent of the payment from a similar annuity that is not indexed. Of course, in later years, the payments from indexed annuities will be much higher than those from regular annuities. Before committing yourself to indexed annuities, you should carefully research all your RRSP retirement income options to ensure that your income needs will be met both now and long into the future.

REGISTERED RETIREMENT INCOME FUNDS

RRIFs have become the most popular RRSP retirement income option over the past decade for good reason. They are extremely flexible and can be customized for virtually anyone's income needs. And with the changes introduced in 1992, RRIFs have become even better. The reasons are many:

- RRIFs offer a built-in inflation protection factor, unless you choose to opt out of it.
- While minimum amounts must be withdrawn from an RRIF each year and be brought into income for tax purposes, you are permitted to withdraw any amount at any time. This is especially valuable if you experience unusual requirements for extra cash in any particular year after you have arranged your retirement income.
- If you stick to the minimum payment schedule from your RRIF, payments will continue well past age 90. In theory, payments will continue for life, but, in fact, the RRIF will be exhausted for all intents and purposes by the time you reach about age 100. This is a considerable improvement over the previous requirement that all amounts be paid out of your RRIF by the time you reach age 90.
- When determining the minimum payment schedule from an RRIF, you can use your spouse's age, if he or she is younger than you, to extend the payments, and also defer your potential tax liability.
- Upon your death, or your spouse's death, all amounts in your RRIF form part of your estate and are available for distribution to your heirs once the appropriate amount of tax is paid. As you approach age 100, less and less will be available since larger minimum payments must be made from the RRIF.
- At any time, you have the option of converting all or a portion of the funds in your RRIF in excess of the minimum withdrawal amount for that year into a life annuity. This will provide a guarantee of payments to you for life, or, if you so opt, to the last

survivor for life of you and your spouse, which, if your family is particularly long-lived, may prove to be attractive.

• RRIFs are similar to RRSPs in that you can control the investment decisions and so have a considerable degree of control over the size of the payments made from the RRIF.

RRIFs have only one significant disadvantage, and this can be overcome. Since you can choose to be responsible for the investing decisions, you may exhaust the funds in your RRIF, and hence reduce or eliminate any payments from it, by making poor investment decisions. You could also impair your RRIF income by simply not paying enough attention to the investments made in your RRIF. This can become a real problem as you get older and financial matters begin to take a back seat to aspects of your retirement that may interest you much more.

This potential problem can be overcome by investing in long-term securities or by buying your RRIF from an issuer that guarantees a specific return on your RRIF funds. The longer the guarantee, however, the less flexibility you generally have with your RRIF. For instance, if you are guaranteed a specific return for ten years and hence a specific income over those years, you may have to forgo the option of being able to withdraw larger amounts from your RRIF at any time of your choosing over those ten years.

RRIFs operate very much like RRSPs, except in reverse. Instead of making contributions to your plan, you must withdraw amounts from it periodically. You can invest your RRSP directly in an RRIF from the issuer, much the same as you would acquire a GIC that is registered as an RRSP. A GIC type of RRIF will carry a specific interest rate for a specific period of time and a certain level of payments will be guaranteed over that period. Alternatively, you may choose to invest in a mutual fund that is a qualified investment for an RRIF (almost all that qualify as investments for RRSPs also qualify as RRIF investments). Or, you may choose to open a self-directed RRIF with your RRSP amounts. Generally, an RRIF may invest in almost all the same investments as an RRSP. As well, all amounts in an RRIF, including the earnings on investments in the RRIF, remain tax-sheltered until amounts are paid out.

As with RRSPs, you may have any number of RRIFs, and amounts in one RRIF may be transferred directly to another RRIF by the issuer, with no adverse tax consequences. Amounts from RRSPs must be transferred directly to your RRIF. You cannot receive the funds. If your RRIF is with the same issuer as your RRSP, it may be a simple matter of re-registering the RRSP as an RRIF.

Minimum RRIF Payments

With the introduction of the extended payment RRIF rules in 1992, it has become somewhat more complicated to determine the minimum payment that must be made from an RRIF each year. Until you reach age 71, the minimum amount is based on the old rules. These state that a specific fraction of the fair market value of the RRIF at the beginning of the year must be paid out before the end of that year. Of course these payments, which must commence in the year immediately after the calendar year in which you purchase the RRIF, must be included in your income for tax purposes in respect of that year. The fraction is determined as follows:

$$\frac{1}{90 \text{ minus your age at the beginning of the year or your spouse's age if so elected}}$$

For example, if you are age 62 at the beginning of the first full year you have an RRIF, and the value of your RRIF (we assume that you have only one RRIF) is $100,000 at the beginning of that year, you must receive an annual payment from the RRIF totalling $3,571. This amount is arrived at as follows:

$$\frac{1}{90 - 62} \times \$100,000 = \frac{1}{28} \times \$100,000 = \$3,571$$

Expressed as a percentage, the fraction is 3.57 per cent. If your spouse is age 59 at the beginning of the year and you elect to use his or her age to determine the relevant fraction (this election must be made before you receive your first payment from the RRIF), the fraction in the first year would be $1/90\text{--}58 = 1/32$ (3.21 per cent). The minimum payment in this case would be $3,125.

These fractions or percentages apply only until the year in which you are age 70 at the beginning of the year. In the next year (the year in which you are age 71 at the beginning of the year) and thereafter, new rules that were proposed in the February 1992 federal budget state that a specific percentage must be used to determine the minimum payment from your RRIF. The percentages are as follows:

Age	Percentage	Age	Percentage
71	7.38	83	9.58
72	7.48	84	9.93
73	7.59	85	10.33
74	7.71	86	10.79
75	7.85	87	11.33
76	7.99	88	11.96
77	8.15	89	12.71
78	8.33	90	13.62
79	8.53	91	14.73
80	8.75	92	16.12
81	8.99	93	17.92
82	9.27	94+	20.00 each year

Several points should be noted about this schedule. First, if you took your first payment at age 62 and used the 3.57 per cent factor, the minimum payment percentage at age 70 would be 5 per cent. However, in the next year (age 71) the percentage would jump to 7.38 per cent, which is higher than it would have been under the old RRIF rules (5.26 per cent). If you were using the minimum percentages each year, possibly because you really had no need for the income, your income would jump considerably in the year when you are 71 at the beginning of the year. There is no other way of deferring income as efficiently as with an RRIF, so you will simply have to live with this jump in the percentage.

However, once you reach age 79, the minimum percentage of your RRIF that must be paid out each year is lower than under the old rules and it continues to be considerably lower for the remainder of the years you are receiving money from your RRIF.

Please note that if you owned an RRIF at the end of 1992, the old schedule of minimum payments applies up to age 78, at which point the new percentage schedule kicks in with its lower percentages.

Of course, under the new rules, these lower payments allow your RRIF, at least in theory, to last indefinitely. The highest minimum payment required is 20 per cent of the fund balance at the beginning of the year the annuitant reaches age 94. However, chances are good at this point that you will begin to exhaust the funds in your

RRIF by taking out 20 per cent each year. In fact, as soon as the earnings rate in your RRIF is no longer greater than the minimum payment percentage, the capital in your RRIF will begin to decline. By the time you reach age 94, it could be seriously depleted and you will find your annual payments declining precipitously.

For example, assume that you still managed to have $100,000 in your RRIF by the time you reached age 94. In the year immediately following (you are 94 at the beginning of that year), you must receive $20,000 from your RRIF (20 per cent of $100,000). Assuming that you receive the payment at the end of the year and your RRIF is earning 8 per cent annually, your next payment will be only $17,600 and the age 96 payment will $15,488. In the year you turn age 100, assuming you are that fortunate, your annual payment from the RRIF will have declined to $9,288 and your RRIF will be worth about $40,868.

This may or may not pose a problem, depending on your expenses, the cost of living, and your other sources of income. Nevertheless, no one likes to see his or her income decline at any age. In other words, even though you may be able to keep your RRIF open indefinitely, it won't necessarily produce the income you expect it to, and on which you have become dependent. It is extremely important that you closely assess cash flow projections from your RRIFs and determine how they fit in with your other sources of retirement income.

Larger RRIF Payments

At any time you may withdraw more than the minimum amount from your RRIF. However, note that withholding tax is payable on any amount withdrawn in excess of the minimum amount. This tax is credited against your tax payable when you report the income in your tax return. Every time you withdraw more than the minimum from your RRIF, you reduce the size of future payments. In fact, if you withdraw considerably more than the minimum each year, you run the risk of draining the funds in your RRIF long before they otherwise would be exhausted. For example, let's assume that you have $100,000 in your RRIF and it is earning about 8 per cent a year. If you receive your first payment in the year you are 65 at the beginning of the year, the minimum amount would be about $4,000. However, let's assume that you take out $15,000 that first year and continue to take out $15,000 each year thereafter. You will discover that your RRIF is devoid of funds within ten years or by the time you are age 75. Chances are that, statistically, you and your spouse will live much longer than this and will no longer be able to depend on the RRIF income.

This scenario highlights the major danger of RRIFs — they will not last forever if you abuse them. It's up to you not to mishandle them. With an annuity, you are generally locked into the payments that are spelled out in your annuity contract. With an RRIF, you may be locked in for a period, if you purchased the kind of RRIF that guarantees payments over a specific period. But after that time, you will be able to choose how to receive your RRIF income. And, of course, if you have a self-directed RRIF or a mutual fund RRIF, you will generally be able to trigger withdrawals any time you desire.

On the other hand, the minimum payment option may offer more inflation protection than you really need. You should definitely investigate a variety of payment options with your RRIF to determine what might be suitable over the next decade or two or three. It will not be too difficult to arrange a payment schedule that allows a reasonable degree of inflation protection but does not threaten to exhaust your RRIF too soon. You should plan to review your choices every year or so, taking account of how much remains in your RRIF and looking at changing economic circumstances.

When you establish your RRIF, it is extremely important that you elect for your spouse to become the annuitant of your RRIF should you die first. If this is not done, the entire amount in the RRIF will be included in your estate at death and be subject to tax before it passes on to your heirs, who may indeed be your spouse. It may be possible for the executor of your estate to elect to have your spouse become the annuitant of the RRIF if he or she is indeed the beneficiary of your estate.

RRSPs AND MARRIAGE BREAKDOWN

On the breakdown of a marriage, funds in one spouse's RRSP may be transferred directly to the other spouse's RRSP on a tax-free basis. This often occurs when one spouse must, under the relevant family law, make an equalization payment to the other spouse. Note that amounts in RRSPs, as well as in RRIFs, of one spouse may also be transferred directly to RRIFs and registered pension plans of the other spouse upon the breakdown of a marriage. To escape tax, such payments must also be made pursuant to a decree, order or judgment of a competent tribunal, or a written separation agreement.

On such transfers, the attribution rules, under which income from assets transferred from one spouse to the other is taxed in the hands of the transferor, not the recipient, do not apply. As well, the rules discouraging the collapsing of spousal RRSPs cease to apply upon the breakdown of a marriage. Spousal RRSPs and the attribution rules are discussed in more detail in Chapter 10.

RRSPs, DEATH, AND EMIGRATION

The treatment of RRSPs and RRIFs upon death is dealt with in more detail in Chapter 11 on estate planning. How RRSPs are taxed when you leave Canada permanently is discussed in Chapter 17.

Chapter 9 — Decisions Facing Owner-Managers

A variety of unique decisions face the owner-manager of a small business when he or she begins to consider the implications of stepping down from the helm of the business and retiring. Owner-manager retirement issues are dealt with at length in the Deloitte & Touche book *Tax Planning for Success: Practical Approaches for You and Your Business*. We'll touch on just a few of the areas in this chapter and highlight some of the planning possibilities.

By "owner-manager", we are referring generally to the owner of an incorporated business, the person who owns a controlling interest in the company and has absolute control over virtually all financial decisions that affect the company and its majority shareholder. Your spouse and/or children may also own shares in the company, but you still exercise control and make the final decisions on all significant matters. As well, you might share ownership and control with one or two other partners, but your financial goals and therefore the decisions you make are compatible.

As an owner-manager, it is likely that your retirement income will come from one or more of the following five sources:

- pension income, from an RRSP, DPSP, or RPP;
- your investment in the business, which will usually take the form of dividends paid on your shares, interest paid on your shareholder loans, the redemption of certain preferred shares, or the repayment by the corporation of debt owing to you;
- the accumulated value of the business accruing to you, which will generally take the form of a capital gain when you sell all or a portion of your shares in the corporation;

- various deferrals that may be available to you as an employee of the business;
- earnings of the business that are deferred or segregated for the express purpose of generating retirement income or facilitating your estate planning objectives, and that are often accumulating in a separate investment company.

As you can see, the bulk of your retirement income may well be derived from your business in one form or another.

Before beginning our overview of retirement income possibilities, we want to point out that any retirement planning the owner-manager undertakes should generally be carried out in concert with an estate and succession planning program. Who succeeds you in the business and the manner in which you wish to accomplish this change in ownership and control, and how you plan to deal with your other assets, will have a large impact on any retirement planning that you are considering. These issues are discussed further in Chapter 12 and also in *Tax Planning for Success.*

RRSP OR RPP?

Owner-managers are allowed to participate in various retirement savings vehicles sponsored by their corporation, such as group RRSPs and defined contribution RPPs, but not DPSPs. They are also allowed to participate in special defined benefit plans called "designated registered pension plans" or DRPPs. As one gets closer to retirement, defined benefit RPPs provide the largest tax deductions for the company and could provide the largest benefits in retirement. Fearing abuse by owner-managers, since they control the plan, the government introduced the concept of the more restrictive DRPP.

Essentially, these are defined benefit plans in which more than 50 per cent of the retirement benefits accruing in the plan go to connected shareholders (persons owning at least 10 per cent of the shares of any class of the employer corporation), persons related to connected shareholders, persons not dealing at arm's length with the corporation, and highly paid employees of the corporation. "Highly paid" means earning at least 2.5 times the current yearly maximum pensionable earnings (YMPE) used in C/QPP calculations and which in 1993 is about $32,500. Using this definition means that a person earning an annual salary of about $81,250 would be "highly paid".

The maximum benefits that can be paid from a DRPP differ slightly from those available from a regular defined benefit RPP. The benefits are calculated as the aggregate of all amounts, each of which is computed for each year of eligible service provided by the owner-manager. These amounts are determined each year as the lesser of:

- $1,722 (indexed annually after 1995), and
- 2 per cent times the updated earnings for the member for the particular year.

An "updated earnings" calculation is used, not a "best average earnings" calculation. The owner-manager must receive remuneration (salary, wages, bonuses, but not dividends) in each year for that year to qualify for a retirement benefit. "Updated earnings" means that the earnings are adjusted to reflect the increase in the average wage index from the particular year in which they are earned to the year in which the owner-manager's pension commences to be paid. The pension benefit that is eventually paid to the owner-manager can be indexed to reflect changes in the Consumer Price Index, thus providing a certain degree of inflation protection.

A number of restrictions apply to DRPPs. Generally, past service benefits for the owner-manager for years prior to 1990 must be approved by Revenue Canada and their present value cannot exceed the present value of all benefits provided to other unrelated active members of any registered pension plan sponsored by the owner-manager's corporation. For years after 1989, owner-manager past service contributions are allowed only to the extent that contributions made to RRSPs or other RPPs by or on behalf of the owner-manager have not been maximized. As well:

- Disability and reduced service benefit funding is restricted.
- Retirement is assumed to be at age 65, so early retirement benefits cannot be pre-funded.
- Surviving spouse benefits are limited to two-thirds of the member's pension at the time of death.

- The guarantee period is limited to fifteen years, but only a five-year guarantee period is allowed if the surviving spouse option is chosen.
- No funding of discretionary pension increases is permitted. The plan must provide for periodic increases as part of the general benefit.
- Once the retirement benefits have been calculated, it is necessary to determine the contribution presently required to fund the benefits promised by the plan. The rules state that in order for the contributions to be deductible, certain actuarial methods and assumptions must be used in the calculation. These rules impose a maximum contribution limit that is primarily based on the age of the owner-manager.

As with a regular RPP, the employer (the owner-manager's corporation) must fund at least one-half the benefits accruing to the owner-manager. The corporation can fund the entire cost of the pension, but generally the decision concerning who makes the contributions depends on the tax rate of the owner-manager and the corporation. The one with the higher rate should maximize his, her, or its contributions.

It should be noted that DRPPs can be expensive to set up and operate each year. As well, they require an actuarial evaluation every three years, which adds to the expense.

IF YOU DON'T HAVE A DESIGNATED RPP (DRPP), SHOULD YOU?

The simple answer is yes, probably. The more complicated answer is, it all depends.

Until recently, most owner-managers were deferring income for retirement with RRSPs or a combination of RRSPs and DPSPs. With the introduction of DRPPs, many "older" owner-managers have opted for the new types of plans. The opportunity to shelter more income, which generally goes hand in hand with the possibility of receiving better benefits upon retirement, has been the main motivating factor. Contributions to both RRSPs and DRPPs hinge on your earned income, which is generally salary and bonuses. RRSP contributions depend on income earned in the previous year, while DRPP contributions depend on future income projected from current levels. Outlined below is a comparison of estimated DRPP contributions with RRSP contributions for owner-managers of various ages who join a DRPP in 1993. The calculations reflect the following broad assumptions:

- The owner-manager is male.
- The maximum pension benefit is to be accrued in each year of service (currently $1,722, indexed after 1995).
- The owner-manager will provide services until he turns age 65, at which time he will retire.
- The retirement benefits will be indexed to increases in the CPI minus 1 per cent.
- The retirement benefits will be guaranteed for at least five years.
- After the death of the owner-manager, the surviving spouse will receive survivor's benefits calculated at two-thirds of the annual benefits received by the owner-manager immediately before death. Survivor's benefits will also be increased annually for increases in the CPI.
- The owner-manager will receive salary in excess of $86,000 in each of 1992 and 1993.

Age	1993 Allowable RRSP Contribution	1993 Allowable DRPP Contribution
30	$12,500	$12,700
35	12,500	13,900
40	12,500	15,300
45	12,500	17,100
50	12,500	18,800
55	12,500	20,200
60	12,500	22,200
65	12,500	27,200

The older you are, the more can be contributed to the DRPP compared with the RRSP because fewer years are available to accumulate the funds necessary to pay the promised pension benefits at age 65. When the DRPP has 35 or more years to generate the funding, smaller amounts need be contributed. Note that owner-managers with a DRPP in this situation can also contribute a maximum of $1,000 to an RRSP each year.

Although considerably more can be contributed to the DRPP the closer you approach age 65, the decision to use one may not be quite so cut and dried, although there are a number of advantages to using a DRPP over an RRSP as you approach retirement age.

- Amounts invested in a DRPP are protected from the creditors of both the corporation and the owner-manager. Of course, the pension benefits payable under the plan can be attacked by creditors, but not until they are actually paid. RRSPs are generally not protected from personal creditors, although using an insurance type of RRSP may offer some protection.
- Interest on money borrowed by the corporation to make DRPP contributions is deductible by the company, while personal borrowing to make DRPP or RRSP contributions is not. Most DRPPs are structured so that the employer makes the bulk of the contributions. Note that the salary paid to the owner-manager to enable him or her to make an RRSP contribution is a deductible expense to the employer, therefore providing an indirect interest deduction for the RRSP contribution if the company borrows to pay the salary.
- Since the employer will be making the bulk, if not all, of the DRPP contributions, the owner-manager will not run into AMT problems with the DRPP. This is not the case with RRSP contributions, which are added back to income for purposes of the AMT.
- Generally, a DRPP can make the same investments that an RRSP can, with one major exception. In some provinces, the DRPP cannot invest in the mortgage on your home. Neither plan is permitted to invest directly or indirectly in your business. If the DRPP's investments do not perform well and a deficiency in the plan arises, the company will be required to fund the deficit to ensure that sufficient funds are in the plan to fund the promised benefits. These extra contributions are deductible to the corporation. If your RRSP performs poorly, no additional contributions are allowed. You will simply end up with reduced benefits on retiring.

Despite the fact that less can be contributed to an RRSP than to a DRPP, the former has a number of advantages that should be considered:

- While the maximum contribution allowed for RRSPs stands at $12,500 in 1993, it is scheduled to rise to $15,500 by 1996, in which year the maximum pension allowable under a DRPP begins to be indexed. The $15,500 RRSP maximum is indexed beginning in 1997. These higher RRSP limits will certainly make the RRSP more attractive in future years than it is now.
- RRSPs are extremely inexpensive to open and maintain. DRPPs are costly in comparison, although the expense is deductible by the employer corporation if it indeed pays the expenses.
- RRSPs are much more flexible than DRPPs. At any time, you can collapse the plan and bring the amounts into income for tax purposes (this is not permitted with locked-in plans). Or you can arrange to convert the RRSPs into a retirement income at any time. And if you are leaving Canada at retirement, you can take the after-tax RRSP lump sum with you to your new country of residence, whereas the DRPP must remain in Canada, although you will still continue to be paid retirement benefits from the plan. While you can arrange an early pension with the DRPP, bear in mind that funding was made on the assumption of retirement at age 65, so your benefits will be reduced considerably.
- An RRSP can invest in the mortgage on your home and the amount received can then be reinvested in your business, which gets around the rule preventing direct investment in your business. This may not be possible with a DRPP. The interest on the mortgage should be deductible if the proceeds are invested in the shares of your company, which in effect gives you a double deduction — once by the corporation when a salary is paid to fund the RRSP contribution and again when interest on the mortgage proceeds is paid.
- If you sell your company before you retire, your RRSP stays intact since it is a personal asset. Your accumulated benefits in a DRPP, on the other hand, may be transferred only to a new DRPP in a new corporation that you control, or, within limits, amounts may also be transferred to your RRSP. Amounts not transferred, such as overfunding, may be returned to you in certain circumstances, after the appropriate amount of tax is paid.
- Contributions to the RRSP are entirely voluntary each year. If

you miss a year, you have at least seven years to make up for the missed contribution. With a DRPP, your company has no choice — contributions must be made every year unless the plan is overfunded. This may not always be in the best interests of your business.

- The RRSP has the potential of providing far better benefits than the DRPP, if its investment performance is stellar. However, if the earnings are less than average, the DRPP should provide better benefits, which, remember, are dictated by the terms of the DRPP.
- With an RRSP, you can make spousal contributions, which means your spouse will receive the retirement benefits and be taxed on them. This could result in significant tax savings. Unless your spouse is an employee of your company, he or she cannot be a member of the DRPP.
- You are allowed to overcontribute to your RRSP up to a cumulative maximum of $8,000. This "overfunding" does not compare with the overfunding that may occur in a DRPP, but it may help provide a slightly improved RRSP retirement income.

Bear in mind that if family members are employees and shareholders of the corporation, they will probably have to go through the same exercise of comparing alternatives, since they will also be allowed to be members of a DRPP or contribute to an RRSP.

Not every owner-manager has the luxury of contributing to a pension plan or RRSP as well as always having adequate financing for the business each and every year. And many others wonder why they should bother contributing to a DRPP or RRSP at all, when they could be investing those funds in the business and perhaps earning a much better return. After all, returns between 20 and 30 per cent year in and year out are not uncommon in successful small businesses, while consistent returns of this magnitude in a DRPP or RRSP would certainly be unusual.

PRACTICAL POINTER   Generally, you will be better off if your return in the DRPP or RRSP is higher than the corporation's after-tax cost of borrowing. Historically, one might expect the rates to be relatively close, if the company is claiming the interest expense against income taxed at the small business rate. If the business is taxed at the highest corporate rate, the advantage definitely swings to the RRSP or DRPP.

Still, many owner-managers feel more comfortable investing in themselves and what they know best, rather than in the usual pension investments. If you can't do both, don't ignore your inclinations and common sense. This is one reason why you have operated a successful business up to now.

PRACTICAL POINTER   If your business is successful, you should not have any trouble borrowing to finance your business. Generally, this should mean that you will be able to provide your business with all the funding it needs and you should be able to maximize your pension contributions. Why not have it both ways?

SPOUSE INVOLVED IN YOUR BUSINESS

If your spouse is involved in your business, you may be able to accumulate more for your retirement years than would otherwise be the case. If your spouse is performing a job that a non-family member would have to perform, the income paid to your spouse stays in the family. However, if your spouse is performing a task that you would otherwise do or other employees would do with no increase in pay, then you will generally not be adding to the family's retirement income accumulations, unless profits of the business improve as a result. However, that income earned by your spouse will be taxed in his or her hands, not in your hands, and any retirement income eventually generated from, for example, an RRSP, will be likewise taxed. If your spouse would otherwise not have produced much retirement income, this should result in a tax saving, since you will likely be taxed at relatively high rates compared with your spouse.

Bear in mind that your spouse must perform duties in the company that are commensurate with the wage being paid. Otherwise, the income could be attributed to you and/or the wage paid will not be allowed as a deduction by the corporation.

INCOME SPLITTING WITH YOUR SPOUSE

Income splitting in general is discussed in more detail in Chapter 10.

Here we will simply hit a few of the highlights of income splitting with a controlled corporation. Income splitting is simply arranging for income that would normally be taxed in your hands at a high rate to instead be taxed in the hands of a family member with a lower rate of tax. As might be expected, the government frowns on income splitting schemes and so has enacted various rules to discourage the practice, called the income attribution rules. In very general terms, these say that if you transfer funds or assets in any way to your spouse, or lend funds to your spouse, all income and capital gains earned by your spouse will be attributed to you and be taxed in your hands. This would include giving or lending your spouse funds to invest in your business.

As well, the corporate attribution rules state that if you lend or transfer funds to the corporation and one of the main purposes of the loan or transfer is to reduce your income and to benefit a family member, the corporate attribution rules will apply. For example, if you lend funds to your business to enable the payment of dividends to your shareholding spouse, the corporate attribution rules may apply.

These rules do not apply if your business is a qualifying small business and the shares of the corporation are eligible for the $400,000 capital gains exemption. This generally means that at least 90 per cent of the fair value of the assets of the business is devoted to earning active business income (as opposed to investment income). The rules will also not apply if your spouse owns less than 10 per cent of the issued shares of all classes. In these cases, you still cannot give your spouse funds to acquire the shares or simply give him or her the shares, because the general income attribution rules would then apply. However, if your spouse has used his or her own funds (earnings, inheritances, gifts from persons other than you) to invest in your business, there is no attribution and your spouse can be paid dividends just as you are.

PRACTICAL POINTER   **If your company was not originally established with your spouse as a shareholder, it may be possible to rearrange the ownership to include your spouse as a shareholder who holds more than 10 per cent of the shares of any one class. Or your spouse can purchase shares of a particular class up to the 9.9 per cent limit in your current corporation, but only if his or her own funds are used. If you are planning a corporate reorganization, professional advice and assistance is absolutely essential.**

DEFERRALS AVAILABLE TO THE OWNER-MANAGER

Some of the income deferrals that are available to employees in general are discussed in Chapter 6. Here we briefly examine a few that are available to owner-managers.

If corporate income exceeds the small business annual limit of $200,000, chances are that you are paying out a bonus equal to the excess amount and perhaps lending it back to the corporation. The bonus must be paid within 180 days of the end of the corporation's fiscal year for it to be deductible by the corporation in the year it is declared.

Interest might be payable on the loan made back to the corporation. You could consider having this interest income eventually form part of your retirement income. As well, the income may solve any AMT and CNIL (cumulative net investment loss — see Chapter 10) problems that you may have. Note that this could be a somewhat risky strategy if you no longer control the company when you finally retire.

If you are taxed at the top marginal rate for individuals and your business is taxed at the small business rate, it could be attractive to retain funds in the company rather than receive them directly as salary or dividends. However, this brings up a host of considerations, all of which may affect your retirement planning. First, if the retained income begins to earn investment income in the corporation, it will be subject to rates of tax that are comparable to personal rates. More seriously, if your business earns significant amounts of investment income, you may not qualify for the $400,000 special capital gains exemption that is available on the sale of shares in qualifying Canadian-controlled private corporations (CCPCs). Furthermore, your income splitting program may be derailed. Of course, if the income is ploughed back into the business or is used to reduce corporate debt, this is not a worry.

MANAGEMENT CONTRACTS

Many owner-managers bow out of their businesses slowly, some because they are reluctant to let go, others because the continued viability of the business demands their expertise, and still others because they need to generate a substantial source of retirement income, at least for the first few years. If you sell your business to outside parties, transfer ownership to your children, or even sell it to key employees, you might consider a management contract that spells out specific duties you are to perform and that allows you to spend as much or as little time as you want with the business after a certain date. This is a common feature of many sale agreements. Both the seller and the purchaser are generally anxious to honour such agreements, since the health of the business may depend on the continued presence of the old owner. You would be especially willing to enter into such an agreement if the sale contract stated that a portion of your proceeds were dependent on the future income of the business, or you were being paid over a period of time out of the company's profits.

CONTINUED OWNERSHIP AND INVOLVEMENT

It's not uncommon for owner-managers to continue to hold shares in their corporations long after they have surrendered controlling interest to their children or an outside purchaser. This type of continued involvement may be advisable if you are receiving the proceeds from the sale of your business over a period of years. However, dividends paid on both common and preferred shares can augment your retirement income. If you are depending on the income, holding preferred shares is desirable, since dividends must be paid on them before dividends can be paid on the common shares held by the new owners. Nevertheless, depending on your old company for a significant portion of your retirement income may not be advisable unless you exercise a degree of both management and real control over the company in the form of voting shares and control on the board of directors.

You may also want to consider lending funds to the corporation or simply not taking out funds that you have already lent to the company. If you are bowing out and no longer will have management or share ownership control, the loan should be secured by fixed assets of the corporation, or perhaps by receivables. There is no point in risking a substantial portion of your retirement capital on new ownership that may not be able to run your old business as profitably as you have done in the past.

THE $400,000 SMALL BUSINESS CAPITAL GAINS EXEMPTION

The $400,000 small business capital gains exemption is available on the sale of shares of a qualifying small business corporation. To qualify, at least 50 per cent of the corporation's assets must have been devoted to an active business in the 24 months preceding the sale of the shares in the corporation; that is, investment activity, as opposed to active business activity, must occupy less than 50 per cent of the corporation's assets. As well, at the time the shares are sold, at least 90 per cent of the corporation's assets must be devoted to an active business.

Each shareholder is entitled to his or her own $400,000 exemption. Thus, if both you and your spouse own shares in the business, you have the potential of realizing up to an $800,000 capital gain tax-free. In addition, your regular $100,000 capital gains exemption applies to any gains arising on the sale of assets, including shares of your corporation.

It goes without saying that you should make every attempt to use this major tax break. This means ensuring that your spouse owns sufficient shares in the company to maximize his or her exemption. But more importantly, it means ensuring that you do not "taint" the company with investment income in the critical period before you plan to sell the shares. A variety of techniques exists for achieving both these ends, even though you may be within a few years of selling and currently your company does not meet the criteria for the exemption.

Transferring investment assets out of your operating company into one that is designed to hold only investments is commonly done. There are no tax consequences, although there is some expense involved in setting up the new company and obtaining the proper professional advice. Similarly, involving your spouse in the ownership of your company may mean setting up a new corporation or reorganizing the share structure of your current company. Again professional advice is essential. A number of techniques and other related matters are discussed in much more detail in the Deloitte & Touche book *Tax Planning for Success*.

Chapter 10 — Other Investments and Financial Strategies

The closer you get to retiring, the more your investment perspective changes. Unfortunately, some of your objectives begin to compete with, rather than complement, each other.

As the countdown continues, the security of your invested capital takes on growing importance. Since this capital will be used to generate a portion of retirement income, you don't want to jeopardize it in any way, or see it erode. You simply don't have the time any longer to make up for financial mistakes or setbacks. At the same time, you probably have become much more interested in deferring income than you were in the past. You've entered your peak earning years, have most of your major expenditures behind you, and likely don't currently need the cash income that your investments may be producing.

The easiest and most common way to defer income tax these days is to accrue unrealized capital gains. Tax is payable only when you sell the underlying investment that is producing these gains. However, investing in capital properties almost always entails incurring considerably more risk than you would by investing in interest-bearing securities such as term deposits or guaranteed investment certificates. Interest on these is taxable each year it is earned, whether or not you actually receive it.

Besides, opting for interest-bearing investments leaves you open to the risk of not keeping up with changes in the cost of living. If you lock yourself into long-term interest-bearing investments and rates rise to levels that we saw in the late 1970s and early 1980s, you may start earning negative returns after figuring in taxes and inflation. In fact, over the long term, it is not that easy to earn a positive rate of return by investing solely in interest-bearing securities.

Is there a solution to your dilemma? Diversifying after you have eliminated all your debt is generally the best answer. Combining security and inflation protection with growth and tax deferrals means that you have to take the good with the bad. And with a little planning, the bad does not have to be all that bad. Taxes can be reduced, which increases inflation protection. Some deferrals can be achieved without sacrificing security to a great degree.

TAXATION OF INTEREST INCOME

Interest income is taxed at full rates, that is, at your marginal rate of tax. For all interest-bearing investments acquired after 1989, you are required to report your interest income each year for tax purposes, whether or not you have received it. The old three-year interest accrual rules apply only to those securities that you acquired before 1989. These require that the income be reported at least every three years. The annual accrual rules catch virtually all securities that have an interest component, including some but not all insurance policies, zero coupon bonds such as strips, and various deferred income arrangements that you may have arranged with your employer. "Exempt" insurance policies are not caught by the accrual rules. Issuers of deferred-interest securities are required to report certain information to you and to Revenue Canada so that you can report the appropriate amount on your tax return.

CANADIAN DIVIDENDS

Opting to invest in the preferred shares of a Canadian corporation may provide you with a steady stream of income, open up the possibility of limited capital gains and, as well, give you a tax break on the dividend income from the shares, since all Canadian dividends receive special tax treatment. The Canadian income tax system is designed to provide a measure of relief to a shareholder who receives a dividend from a Canadian corporation, because the dividend is, theoretically, paid out of earnings that have been subjected to tax at the corporate level. For individuals, this relief comes in the form of the dividend tax credit. Essentially, the dividend tax credit acts to reduce personal federal and provincial tax on the dividend. Foreign dividends do not receive this preferential treatment.

An example will show how the dividend tax credit mechanism works. It is assumed that you are in the top tax bracket and a Canadian dividend of $1,000 is received:

Cash amount of dividend	$1,000
Gross-up (25%)	250
	$1,250
Federal tax (29%)	$ 363
Less dividend tax credit (16-2/3% of cash amount)	(167)
	196
Add federal surtaxes	20
Provincial tax (assumed to be 55%)	108
Total tax	$ 324
Amount retained after tax	$ 676

If this $1,000 had been received as interest income, the tax rate would have been close to 50 per cent in most provinces, leaving only a bit over $500 in the pocket of the investor. The tax rate on dividends for individuals in the middle and lower tax brackets is correspondingly lower.

PRACTICAL POINTER   Note that if you have no dependants, you can receive approximately $24,000 in dividends from Canadian corporations in 1993 and pay no tax, assuming that you had no other sources of income in the year.

CAPITAL GAINS AND LOSSES

Capital gains or losses arise when you dispose of a capital asset and the proceeds you receive, net of your selling costs, are higher or lower than your cost of the property. Only three-quarters of a capital gain is subject to tax. And only three-quarters of a capital loss can be applied against the taxable portion of capital gains. If a capital loss cannot be used in the current year, it can be carried back three years or be carried forward indefinitely. Capital losses are denied if you sell property to a corporation controlled by you or your spouse, to your RRSP or your spouse's, or to your RRIF. You also are denied losses if you sell a capital property and then you, your spouse, or a corporation controlled by you or your spouse acquires an identical asset either 30 days before or 30 days after disposing of the original asset.

Generally, the costs of acquiring a capital property are added to the cost base of the property. Costs of selling capital properties are deducted from the proceeds. Both reduce your gain or increase your loss. The amounts are not deductible for tax purposes when incurred. The costs of identical or similar capital properties that have been acquired after 1971 must be grouped together for purposes of establishing a cost base that is the average of the group. As individual assets are sold, the total cost base of the group of assets will be reduced. Special rules apply to capital property acquired by you or a related person before 1972.

A specific type of loss, known as a business investment loss, receives special tax treatment. These are losses incurred on the disposition (deemed or actual) of shares in a "small business corporation" (discussed later in this chapter) or on the disposition or write-off of most forms of debt owed to you by a small business corporation or by a corporation that was a small business corporation when it became bankrupt or was wound up. Three-quarters of a business investment loss may be applied to reduce income for tax purposes from any source and is treated the same as an ordinary business loss. Thus, it may be carried back three years and forward seven years, after being used to reduce your income to zero in the year the loss was incurred. Note that using business investment losses affects your access to the $100,000 capital gains exemption (see below) and the $400,000 small business gains exemption (see Chapter 12).

$100,000 CAPITAL GAINS EXEMPTION

With a couple of exceptions, the $100,000 capital gains exemption applies to gains arising from the disposition of all capital property, including foreign property, by individuals who are Canadian residents. The exemption is cumulative up to a lifetime maximum of $100,000. The exemption is available net of any capital losses claimed in the year, and it is also affected by any business investment losses that you have realized either in the current year or in any prior year back to 1985. Most importantly, it is reduced by any cumulative net investment losses (CNILs) that you have accumulated (see later in this chapter). Note that the maximum deduction for the exemption is actually $75,000, since only three-quarters of a $100,000 capital gain ($75,000) is taxable.

Several points concerning the $100,000 exemption should be borne in mind. First, if an amount is claimed as a deduction, you may become subject to the alternative minimum tax (AMT).

PRACTICAL POINTER   In some cases, there may be no point in claiming the $100,000 capital gains exemption if you are also going to be subject to the AMT. You should first compare tax positions before committing yourself to claiming a deduction for the full amount of the exemption for which you are eligible.

Second, you and your spouse are each entitled to your own $100,000 capital gains exemptions. If your spouse does not currently own capital properties that may eventually generate capital gains, you should carefully read the pages in this chapter on income splitting to ensure that he or she begins to accumulate assets to take advantage of the deduction.

Third, if you are the controlling shareholder of a holding company that owns your portfolio investments, bear in mind that the $100,000 capital gains exemption is available only to individuals. Capital gains realized inside the corporation are subject to tax without the benefit of the $100,000 exemption. Even when you eventually wind up your corporation, it is unlikely that a capital gain will result on the redemption of your shares. As a result, you will not be entitled to the exemption on a wind-up of your corporation.

PRACTICAL POINTER   If you are in any danger of not using up your $100,000 capital gains exemption in the near future because gains are being realized in your investment corporation, and your shares in the corporation have sizeable accrued gains, you might consider reorganizing the

share capital of the company so that the gains are realized. This tactic requires competent professional advice.

Fourth, rumours have been flying for a number of years that the exemption will be eliminated by the federal government. So far, it has been eliminated only for new real estate purchases and is being phased out for gains on real estate owned before March 1992 (see Chapter 14). However, the government could change its mind at any time and further restrict the use of the exemption, or repeal the tax break altogether.

PRACTICAL POINTER **If you have assets with large inherent capital gains, consider crystallizing them to take advantage of the exemption. Selling the assets to a third party will cause the gains to be realized for tax purposes. But you also might want to consider selling the assets to a corporation that you control. The assets stay under your control, but you get to use your $100,000 capital gains exemption. As well, the cost base of the assets is bumped up to a higher value, which will reduce the amount of gain that will be taxed when the assets are eventually sold to a third party.**

As explained in Chapter 13, the principal residence exemption protects the gains on your family home, so it is usually not necessary to use the $100,000 capital gains exemption when you sell your home. However, the principal residence exemption is available on only one home for any particular year, so the $100,000 exemption may be used for the sale of a second home. Note that if you are selling a second home located in the United States or certain other jurisdictions, special taxes might apply (see Chapter 14).

CUMULATIVE NET INVESTMENT LOSSES (CNILs)

The CNIL rules have been in effect since 1988. Essentially, they say that the net capital gains eligible for your capital gains exemption in any year must be reduced by the amount in your CNIL account at the end of that year. Your CNIL at the end of a year is essentially the amount by which your accumulated investment expenses exceed your accumulated investment income. Your investment expenses include the aggregate of the following items that have been deducted from income since 1988:

- interest expense, safety deposit box fees, and other carrying charges claimed in respect of the purchase or holding of investments;
- a variety of limited partnership expenses and losses, and other tax shelter claims;
- 50 per cent of your share of deductions attributed to a resource flow-through share or relating to Canadian exploration and other resource expenses of a partnership where you are not actively engaged in the business;
- any loss from any property, including the rental or leasing of real property.

The CNIL rules do not affect the deductibility of these items for tax purposes. They only affect claims for your $100,000 capital gains exemption, if you have not exhausted it.

Investment income generally consists of the aggregate of the following items included in your income since 1988:

- interest income, taxable dividends, rent and other income from investment properties;
- income from limited partnerships and other tax shelters;
- 50 per cent of recovered exploration and development expenses included in income;
- the income portion of certain annuity payments;
- the amount of certain capital gains not eligible for the exemption.

The CNIL rules do not permanently erode your exemption; they simply delay your access to it.

The following example shows how the CNIL rules work. Assume that you have never realized any capital gains or losses, nor have you reported any property income or loss items. In 1993 you borrow $5,000 to acquire shares which cost $5,000. You sell the shares a year later for $6,000. Your interest expense over that year is $450. Your capital gain on the sale is $1,000 of which $750 is taxable and, but for the CNIL rules, would all be eligible for your $100,000 capital gains exemption. However, the $450 interest expense is added to your CNIL account. Thus, the $750 taxable capital gain eligible for the exemption is reduced by the $450, so only $300 of the taxable gain is tax-free. Tax must be paid on the other $450. However, at the end of the year, you will have eliminated your CNIL problem since you have used the full balance of $450 to offset a portion of your capital gain.

Note that your CNIL account is calculated on a cumulative basis for all items since 1988. If you incurred some interest expense in 1989, $1,300 for example, and have not reported any other investment income since then, nor claimed anything under your $100,000 capital gains exemption, this $1,300 must be added to your CNIL, for a total of $1,750 ($1,300 plus $450). In this case, none of the $750 taxable gain realized in 1993 would be eligible for your exemption, and you would still have a $1,000 CNIL problem at the beginning of 1994.

PRACTICAL POINTERS
- If you own or run a business personally, consider borrowing for business purposes, rather than for investment purposes. Interest on business borrowing is not included in your CNIL account. You might also consider making certain investments through a corporation if you control one, although bear in mind that the $100,000 capital gains exemption is not available on capital gains realized by a corporation.
- A CNIL problem can be eliminated or alleviated before the end of the year if you receive taxable dividends. Thus, if you control a corporation that has earnings, and dividends are paid by the corporation, these will qualify as investment income and reduce any CNIL you might have. Alternatively, if you have lent funds to your corporation on a non-interest-bearing basis, changing the terms of the loan so that interest is charged on the outstanding balance will also produce investment income in your hands. Of course, there is cost involved with this planning. You must report the amounts as income for tax purposes, although the corporation will be allowed a deduction for the interest paid on the loan.

DEDUCTING INTEREST

Interest on borrowed money is deductible for tax purposes if the borrowed funds are used to earn investment income or income from a business. It is not essential that you earn positive income; you simply have to have a reasonable expectation of profit when you invest the borrowed funds. Incurring a loss does not prejudice your ability to claim interest expense deductions. However, if you knew in advance that your rate of return on your investment would be less than your borrowing rate, a portion of your interest expense may be denied as a deduction.

Interest is deductible only if you continue to own the asset. If you sell it and do not repay the loan with the proceeds from the sale, the interest is no longer deductible, even though you may have incurred a loss on the sale and the proceeds are not sufficient to repay the loan. If you purchase another investment with the proceeds, only the portion of the interest expense that relates to the new investment is deductible.

PRACTICAL POINTER   **If you must incur debt, you should always try to borrow for investment or business purposes, and avoid borrowing for personal needs. The interest expense on personal borrowing is not deductible for tax purposes. For example, there is no point in borrowing to take a vacation and using your savings to invest in the stock market.**

DIVERSIFYING FOR BEST RESULTS

As mentioned earlier, diversifying your investments is the best way to achieve your goals as you near retirement. With a reasonably diversified mix of investments, you should be able to:

- use your $100,000 capital gains exemption relatively quickly;
- get rid of losing investments, which should help to reduce your tax burden if you are no longer able to claim the $100,000 capital gains exemption;
- defer gains to your retirement years on the winners that you have in your portfolio; and
- depend on a steady stream of income from your interest- and dividend-bearing investments. This income may allow you to defer receiving a portion of your pension, if possible, or you may be able to leave your RRSP alone until you turn age 71, rather than having to use it immediately after you retire.

TAX SHELTERS

Do tax shelters have a place in the retirement income plans of Canadians? The answer is yes and no. Tax shelters should be steered clear of if you still haven't managed to accumulate sufficient assets to see you and your spouse through your retirement years. Shelters by their very nature are risky and are not liquid, and, while generally delivering on the tax write-offs they promise, don't as often deliver on the income. What you are interested in at this point is accumulating assets that will deliver a steady and attractive income once you retire.

On the other hand, if your retirement funding is under control, and your current earnings from all sources are such that you have much more than you need and consequently are paying much more tax than you would like to be paying, you might consider investigating some of the less risky tax shelters. The stress here is on less risk. There is no point in risking what you have managed to accumulate so far, simply to save a few tax dollars. For one thing, if your income is at that level and you have taken care of your retirement funding, your tax rate isn't likely to change once you retire. If you are in the top tax bracket, you'll probably stay there once you retire. So you may be saving tax dollars now, but the tax you pay a few years down the road will be at the same rate. The deferral definitely is economically worthwhile, but only if you are truly deferring tax. This means that you must invest in a low-risk shelter that will deliver on its income promises.

Unfortunately, there are precious few such shelters available today. Resource-based investments were and continue to be high risk. The write-offs are attractive, but if you are investing in a speculative drilling venture, there is obviously no guarantee of any future income or appreciation in the value of your shares in the project.

Investing in film and video tapes may expose you to the same kind of risk, although it is possible to limit your risk with certain investments. For example, a few children's television programs are structured as tax shelters and offer relatively firm guarantees of future profits. It is also possible to invest in the advertising for feature films, and be assured that at least a portion of your investment will be returned to you. Your investment is 100 per cent deductible in the year it is made and, generally, such investors are the first to share in the profits from the film, which only needs to be moderately successful to ensure some return on your investment.

Real estate has had its ups and downs lately, and is not a good investment outside of a few areas in the country, although some foreign areas may represent better value. Up-front deductible costs for real estate investing have been drastically curtailed over the years; the write-off of operating losses on your investment is restricted; and the potential for being able to sell your investment, even at a loss, is questionable in today's market, except in a few selected areas.

Investing in yachts or recreational vehicles should be considered reasonably high risk, although, if you invest with a promoter with a long-term successful track record, you may enjoy a positive cash flow fairly quickly, with moderate but not spectacular write-offs. Many of these deals let you use your investment for a few weeks each year.

There are few research and development (R&D) tax shelters being put into place, although that might change with the new, slightly more liberalized R&D rules that were announced recently by the government. However, the restrictions on limited partnership write-offs may reduce the attractiveness of new issues. Note that several provinces, including Ontario and Quebec, also offer R&D incentives, which may encourage shelters to be offered in those provinces.

LIMITED PARTNERSHIP MUTUAL FUND SHELTERS

Currently one of the least risky, and therefore most attractive tax shelters around, is a limited partnership mutual fund shelter. The money you invest in the limited partnership goes to pay commissions to the brokers and others who sell the units in a mutual fund. These are typically back-end load funds that charge a redemption fee when units in the fund are eventually sold by an investor. The longer the units are held, the lower the redemption fee. At some point, no fee is charged to the mutual fund investor upon redemption of the units.

The sales period for the limited partnership investment is fixed. If sufficient shares in the mutual fund have not been sold at the end of the period, a portion of your investment is returned. You earn income through the redemption fees collected and, as well, you receive a portion of the monthly administration fee charged by the manager of the fund. Generally, the investment is structured so that you can write off a large portion of your actual cash investment in the first year.

These shelters are attractive in that your downside is protected. If the fund performs well and the value of its shares increases, there are fewer redemptions but your income from the administration fee increases. If the fund does poorly, your administration fee income declines but your redemption fee income increases as investors sell more and more of their shares in the fund. You will do better in the long run if the fund performs well and most of your income is in the form of the administration fee.

You will likely begin to earn income in the year after investing in the limited partnership, and this income stream will, in theory, continue indefinitely, unless all the shares related to your investment are redeemed. Thus, this type of tax shelter investment may be attractive for those who are looking for a tax write-off in the few years before retiring and who also want to augment their retirement income. However, the investments are not without risk. The mutual fund share issue may not sell out and you may have tied up a portion of your investment for up to a year and get little or nothing back in return. The mutual fund manager also may not do well with the fund, which means that most of your income will be in the form of redemptions. This doesn't produce nearly as attractive a return as if you were receiving administration fees for a period of years.

No matter how you invest, you should ensure that you get qualified and competent professional advice. Tax shelters are complex investments that could lead to tax results you would never have expected. Don't lose sight of the fact that despite the write-offs offered, you are still putting at least 50 cents on the dollar at risk. And watch out for deals that, for example, promise write-offs for a $10,000 investment but require that you put only $1,000 into the deal. You are borrowing the rest in some fashion and are on the hook for that borrowing. Above all, investigate the promoter of any deal. For example, it should be quite easy to explore the track record of any mutual fund putting together a limited partnership arrangement, and to compare this fund with several others offering the same type of deal in prior years.

IS THERE ANY POINT IN SETTING UP A HOLDING COMPANY?

Many individuals with relatively large portfolios of investments have, at one time or another, thought about incorporating those investments. Establishing a separate holding company to own your investments can make sense, but only in some situations. Setting up Holdco, our name for your investment corporation, may result in a deferral of tax to future years and it may facilitate your estate planning program if your children become involved with the corporation.

However, be aware that creating Holdco does not guarantee that you will actually save any tax in the long run. In fact, there is currently no significant difference between earning income through a corporation and earning it personally. However, the corporation will cost you money to set up and there will likely be an annual expense associated with the up-keep of the company. In other words, you may be better off financially by not setting up the company, unless the tax deferral works to your advantage.

First, let's take a brief look at how Holdco is taxed. Interest income is taxed at full corporate rates, as are three-quarters of any capital gains realized by the corporation. The federal corporate rate of tax is 28.8 per cent, including the 3 per cent surtax. Provincial rates vary, but average around 15 per cent, which means the corporate rate on interest and taxable capital gains is about 44 per cent. The personal rate on this income varies from province to province but averages about 50 per cent. Thus, there is a small deferral of, on average, about six percentage points if the income is earned in the corporation instead of being earned personally.

To get money out of the corporation, it must pay its shareholders a dividend. We won't go through the mechanics — they are complex and, unless you see how the whole corporate tax system works, they don't make a lot of sense — but suffice to say that the total tax on the investments is about the same whether earned personally or through the corporation. Due to differences in provincial tax rates and the introduction of federal surtaxes, this tax neutrality may not be exact. You should have your professional advisor run through some possible scenarios to see exactly what the effect is for your particular circumstances. Note that the untaxed portion of any capital gain realized by Holdco can be paid out as a special tax-free capital dividend. This means that it is received tax-free by the shareholder.

Dividends received by Holdco from companies with which it is not connected are taxed at a flat rate of 25 per cent. This tax is refunded in full to Holdco if a dividend is paid, so essentially, the entire pre-tax amount of these dividends is paid to shareholders and taxed in their hands, just as if they had received the dividends directly. The top tax rate on dividends earned personally ranges from about 32 to 37 per cent, depending on the province in which you live. Thus, the deferral available on dividends earned in the corporation and kept there is a bit higher, up to 12 percentage points (25 per cent corporate rate versus 37 per cent personal rate).

To set up the company, you would incorporate it and then issue yourself common shares in exchange for your personally held assets that are transferred into the corporation. This transfer can be done at fair market value, or you may elect to make the transfer at any amount between the cost and the fair market value of the transferred assets. Note that losses are not allowed when a transfer is made to your own corporation, but you can realize capital gains. These gains may be eligible for your $100,000 capital gains exemption.

PRACTICAL POINTER Since the corporation is not eligible for the exemption and the exemption may have a limited life, depending on future legislation, you should consider making sufficient transfers at fair market value to trigger enough gains to use up your $100,000 capital gains exemption. The result will be that Holdco will own these assets with a higher cost base, thus reducing the gain upon an eventual disposition to a third party. Your shares in Holdco will also have a higher cost base.

It's essentially not possible to use an investment corporation for income splitting with your spouse, although the corporation is ideally suited to split income with your adult children and/or accomplish several of your estate planning goals. Generally, your children would establish the corporation and they would own all the common shares. You would transfer your portfolio investments into the corporation and take back voting preferred shares as consideration with a value equal to the fair market value of the portfolio investments. All future capital appreciation of the investments would now belong to the children, since they own the common shares. However, you would retain control of the corporation through your voting preferred shares and you would participate in the income earned by the investments through dividends paid on those preferred shares. Note that the transfer can be made at fair market value, or at any amount between cost and fair market value, as long as the appropriate election is made. If the transfer is made at fair market value, however, this may entail a significant tax cost, particularly if you have already used up your $100,000 capital gains exemption.

If you attempt the same type of arrangement, except that your spouse becomes the owner of at least 10 per cent of the outstanding common shares of Holdco, you may be caught by the attribution rules. In general terms, these say that on such a transfer of assets to a corporation, you must receive a specified minimum return on the amount transferred, based on the prescribed interest rate set by the government every three months. The return can be in the form of dividends on your shares or interest payable by the corporation on a loan. If you do not receive this amount from the corporation, you will be deemed to have earned interest income equal to the minimum amount which must be included in your income for tax purposes. This could result in double taxation.

These attribution rules do not apply if your spouse invests in your small business corporation. Essentially, a small business corporation is one in which at least 90 per cent of the assets of the business are devoted to activities other than investments. For a more detailed discussion, refer to the Deloitte & Touche book *Tax Planning for Success.* You should also have a look at Chapters 9 and 12 of this book.

These rules will generally defeat the whole purpose of trying to get income into the hands of your spouse that otherwise would be taxed in your hands. The only way to involve your spouse in the ownership of Holdco is for him or her to own less than 10 per cent of the shares of any class, which, if your portfolio investments are large, could still generate substantial amounts of income.

PRACTICAL POINTER   Alternatively, after the assets are transferred into Holdco, you could arrange for your spouse to acquire shares of Holdco from you at fair market value. Your spouse must use his or her own funds for the purchase, that is, the funds cannot be given or lent interest-free to him or her by you. Of course, the corporation is not necessary for this transaction. Your spouse could simply acquire some of your portfolio investments directly from you.

INCOME SPLITTING WITH YOUR SPOUSE

As you can tell from the discussion above, income splitting is the process of shifting income that would normally be taxed in your hands into the hands of another family member, such as your spouse. You would like to split the family income because you may have a higher rate of tax than your spouse. For example, if you are taxed at the top rate but your spouse is taxed at the lowest rate, the difference might be as much as 23 percentage points, depending on the province in which you live. Saving 23 cents on every dollar of investment income that you earn is certainly attractive and should prompt you to investigate methods of ensuring that your spouse earns some of that income that would otherwise be taxed at the high rate.

Of course, the Income Tax Act contains a variety of rules to discourage income splitting with your spouse, minor children, and other related persons. We'll just look at the spousal rules. These essentially say that if you loan or transfer property of any kind, in any manner to, or for the benefit of your spouse or a spousal trust, any income earned on the transferred or lent funds, or capital gains realized or losses incurred, will be attributed to you and be taxed in your hands instead of in the hands of your spouse. Nevertheless, since your spouse has received the income, it now belongs to him or her, even though you may be paying the tax. Any income or gains attributed back to you retain their character and therefore gains are eligible for the $100,000 capital gains exemption and Canadian taxable dividends are eligible for the dividend tax credit. Note that the attribution rules continue to apply to property that is substituted for the property originally transferred. However, attribution stops if you, the transferor, die or cease to be a resident of Canada, or if your marriage breaks down.

There are a number of exceptions to the attribution rules and many ways of ensuring that they don't apply. Some require careful planning and most are only effective after they have been in operation over a period of years.

Fair Market Value Sales

The attribution rules do not apply if your spouse buys an asset from you at fair market value. In other words, you have to receive consideration equal to the fair market value of the asset. For a fair market value transfer to take place, the seller must make an election in his or her tax return for the "transfer at cost" rules not to apply. These rules say that when you transfer property to your spouse, it automatically happens at cost unless the election is made. More importantly, your spouse must use his or her own funds to make the purchase from you. You cannot have given your spouse the funds, and if you lend the funds to him or her, you must charge interest on the loan at a reasonable rate that reflects commercial rates at the time the loan is made or is equal to the government's prescribed rate. The interest on the loan must be paid during the year or within 30 days of the end of the year, otherwise the attribution rules will apply.

PRACTICAL POINTER   **If you lend funds to your spouse, you will generally charge the prescribed rate of interest on the loan. Generally, you can determine movements in the prescribed interest rate about two months before the change because of the way the prescribed rate is determined each quarter. Thus, before locking into a longer term on the loan, check out the prescribed rate to see if it is going to decline the next time it is due to be revised.**

Business Income Not Attributable

Business income earned by your spouse using property given or lent by you does not result in attribution. Thus, if your spouse owns his or her own business or wants to start one up, you can give or lend funds to your spouse and any future business income earned will not be taxed in your hands. The business must be an unincorporated one or a partnership in which your spouse actively participates.

If your spouse uses the loan or gift to invest in shares of a corporation that your spouse controls, he or she will be earning investment income (dividends on the shares) which will be attributed back to you. Similarly, if your spouse lends funds to the controlled corporation, then interest, not business income, will be earned on the loan, and this interest will be subject to the attribution rules. As well, if you lend or give funds to your spouse to invest in a limited partnership, such as is used in a tax shelter investment, any resulting income or gains will be subject to the attribution rules.

Note that capital gains resulting from the loan or transfer remain attributable. In other words, if your spouse sells the business at a profit, a portion of the capital gain could be attributable to you and you may incur a tax liability.

Paying Your Spouse a Salary

You may pay your spouse a salary for work performed in an unincorporated business and deduct the salary when calculating your income from the business. If the business is incorporated, the corporation deducts the salary for corporate tax purposes. The amount paid to your spouse must be reasonable in relation to the duties performed. By receiving a salary, your spouse will be in a position to make RRSP contributions, join the company pension plan if there is one, and contribute to the Canada or Quebec Pension Plan.

Spousal Business Partnerships

If you own an unincorporated business, you may want to consider establishing a spousal business partnership if your spouse is to become involved in the business. Documentation of the partnership agreement is a must, especially if you have been running the business for some time. Consideration should be given to the amount of time the spouse spends in the business and his or her capital contribution to the business. If the tax authorities consider the division of partnership profits to be unreasonable, they have the power to reallocate these profits. Generally, if the contribution of capital by a spouse is to be significant, it will be more beneficial to establish a spousal partnership than to pay your spouse a salary.

PRACTICAL POINTER   If your unincorporated business is a sideline, you have other sources of income, and profits from the business won't be realized for a period of time, you may be better off paying your spouse a salary. This will be a deductible expense for the business, and the resulting losses from the business can be used to reduce your other sources of income.

Spousal Registered Retirement Savings Plans

RRSPs were discussed at length in Chapter 8. As noted there, you are eligible to make a spousal contribution at your choosing. It's a simple matter of letting the administrator of your spouse's RRSP know that the contribution you are making to his or her plan is a spousal contribution. The amount you contribute is deductible from your income for tax purposes. Be sure that you make the payment directly to the trustee and receive a tax receipt that says you have made a spousal contribution. Be aware that the total contributions you make to all RRSPs, yours and your spouse's, cannot exceed your personal RRSP limits.

The advantage of contributing to a spousal RRSP is that the amount contributed and the investment income generated in the plan belong to your spouse and will eventually be taxed in his or her hands. Spousal RRSPs are most beneficial if you anticipate that your spouse will have a lower tax rate than you upon retiring.

Note that special rules prevent you making a spousal contribution and then quickly arranging for your spouse to withdraw the amount. Any funds withdrawn by your spouse from a spousal RRSP can be attributed to you and be taxed in your hands if you contributed to any spousal RRSP during the current year or in one of the two immediately preceding years.

Interest on Interest

If your spouse earns interest on the interest generated from funds lent or given to him or her, this is not caught under the attribution rules. In other words, if you give your spouse $10,000 that earns 10 per cent interest, only $1,000 interest on the original $10,000 will be attributed to you each year. The interest earned by your spouse on the $1,000 and all future compounding or reinvested interest will be taxed in your spouse's hands. Over a relatively short period of time, this interest can add up to significant amounts if sizeable sums are initially lent to or given to your spouse.

Pay Your Spouse's Taxes

There is no attribution if you give money to your spouse and it is used to pay his or her income tax, because there is no income earned on the amount. Your spouse then would be able to invest the funds that otherwise would have gone to pay the tax, and this investment income will be taxed in his or her hands. This arrangement does not work if tax is withheld from your spouse's income at source.

Pay the Family Expenses

If you and your spouse are in different tax brackets, the higher-income spouse should pay all the family expenses, while the lower-income spouse should use his or her funds for investment purposes. The investment income will be taxed in that spouse's hands at the lower rate. In the same vein, the higher-income spouse should consider paying off the other spouse's personal loans and credit card debt and making the spouse's insurance payments. Insurance payments may be caught by the attribution rules if the policy is of an investment income type.

Gift Interest Expense to Your Spouse

For the attribution rules to apply, income must be earned or capital gains must be realized. If your spouse has borrowed funds on his or her own account, and you pay the interest owing on the loan, there should be no attribution of any income earned by your spouse in respect of the borrowed funds. If you pay off the principal on your spouse's loan, the attribution rules will apply.

Leveraging Transferred Funds

If you give or lend funds to your spouse, your spouse may be able to borrow a considerably larger sum on his or her own account. Only the income earned on the amount transferred from you would be attributable, while the income earned on the leveraged or borrowed funds would be earned by the spouse and be taxed in his or her hands. Note that you cannot guarantee the loan in any way, otherwise the attribution rules will apply to the full amount of the income.

Optional Payment of Interest

If you lend your spouse funds, interest does not have to be paid until 30 days after the end of the year. Thus, if you lend funds to your spouse at the beginning of January, he or she will earn 13 months of income on the funds before interest must be paid, which ensures that the attribution rules do not apply. If the investment does not pan out over those 13 months, you might consider not having the interest paid. In this case, only the income earned on the investment, if any, would be attributed to you. Note that once you choose this course of action, the attribution rules continue to apply to that particular loan. If your spouse sells the investment and repays the loan, the attribution rules will cease to apply. A new loan could then be made and the process repeated.

Purchase from Your Spouse

There are no rules that prevent one spouse from selling assets to the other at fair market value. Thus, you might consider acquiring assets that are owned by your spouse at their fair market value and paying your spouse cash for the asset. Your spouse must own the asset outright. That is, you cannot have transferred it to, or bought it for, him or her. This technique works best with assets your spouse brought into the marriage, assets bought with money your spouse earned, or assets inherited or bought with money inherited. For example, there is no prohibition on a husband buying his wife's jewellery that she inherited from her grandmother and lending the jewellery to the wife to wear whenever she wants to.

Instead of using cash for the purchase, bear in mind that you can simply swap assets. Thus, if you own shares in a company, you can use these shares as consideration for your spouse's assets that you intend to purchase. Note that you and your spouse will each be disposing of these assets and may realize a gain if the election discussed earlier is made.

Option to Purchase a Valuable Asset

Depending on the nature of the asset, this idea may make sense only if you are a few years away from retiring or you have an asset that will increase fairly rapidly in value. Essentially, you would sell your spouse an option to purchase the asset. Your spouse would exercise the option only if the value of the asset increases substantially. To finance the purchase, your spouse may have to sell the asset.

For example, assume that you own an interest in a race horse that has respectable blood lines and is just about to enter its first race. You bought the interest in the horse for $2,000 and recently you have been offered $5,000 for it. You sell your spouse an option to purchase the horse for its current fair market value of $5,000. The option itself comes with a price tag, say $500, that your spouse pays to you. You should ascertain beforehand what such an option would go for in the marketplace. The option agreement requires that your spouse exercise the option within three years or it expires.

In the real world, chances are that your horse will not perform particularly well in its first few races and the market value of your interest will decline. In this case, your spouse will not exercise the option and you will have made an unfortunate investment.

However, let's assume that the horse does perform well, and, as a three-year old, it wins the Queen's Plate, Canada's premier stakes race. The fair market value of your interest in the horse climbs quickly to $50,000 (you have only a small interest in the beast). Your spouse would then exercise the option, using his or her own funds to pay you the former fair market value of $5,000. At that point, the interest in the horse may be sold, or the interest may be kept if it looks like it will continue to be a worthwhile investment.

At the time you grant the option to your spouse, you would have to include the $500 option price as a capital gain in your income for tax purposes for that year. In the year the option is exercised, you would treat the $500 option price as part of your proceeds; thus, you will be deemed to have received $5,500 in the year the horse is sold. Since you paid $2,000 for the interest in the horse, you will have a capital gain of $3,500, which should be eligible for your $100,000 capital gains exemption. You would also tell Revenue Canada to reassess your return to exclude the $500 capital gain from income in the year the option was granted. The interest in the horse now belongs to your spouse. If the interest is sold for $50,000, the proceeds belong to your spouse and the resulting capital gain ($45,000) is taxed in his or her hands. There is no attribution of any capital gains to you. As your spouse earns income on the $50,000, there will continue to be no attribution.

Sharing CPP Benefits

Bear in mind that when you retire, you can apply to have your Canada Pension Plan (CPP) benefits split with your spouse. Your spouse's benefits must also be split. If you both are entitled to maximum CPP benefits, there is no point making the election. However, if the higher-income spouse's benefits are much larger than the other spouse's CPP benefits, splitting CPP benefits should lower your tax bill a bit during your retirement years. Currently, this option is not available in Quebec.

Leaving Canada

Also bear in mind that the attribution rules cease to apply once you become a non-resident of Canada. A judicious transfer of assets may result in a lower tax bill in the final Canadian tax return that you file. Professional advice is essential and your planning should start well in advance of the date you plan to leave the country.

FOREIGN INVESTMENT INCOME

It is beyond the scope of this book to dwell in any depth on income earned by a Canadian resident from a foreign jurisdiction. We will just highlight a few of the basic concepts with which you should be familiar.

For Canadian tax purposes, you are taxable on your worldwide income while a resident of Canada. Generally, any income taxes you pay to a foreign government on investment or business income earned in that jurisdiction are creditable against your Canadian taxes. You receive a foreign tax credit equal to the lesser of the foreign taxes paid (up to 15 per cent of the foreign income) and the proportion of Canadian tax owing on the income. Foreign taxes paid on foreign investment income are not allowed as a credit against Canadian tax owing on other sources of income. If the amount of foreign taxes paid is greater than the allowable foreign tax credit, you may be able to deduct the excess from your income. Although this is not as beneficial as an actual reduction of Canadian taxes, it does provide some measure of relief.

Generally, countries with which Canada has a tax treaty deal with income earned by a Canadian resident more favourably than non-tax treaty countries. For example, the withholding rate on investment income in the United States is 15 per cent, not the standard 25 per cent. However, this special rate applies only to certain income. In many instances, business income will be taxed at normal U.S. corporate rates, and rates of estate tax and withholding on gambling winnings may be much higher than 15 per cent. As well, Canada allows a credit only on foreign taxes that would be paid in Canada if that income were earned or the transaction took place in Canada. For example, no credit is given for estate tax paid in the United States, or for withholding tax on gambling winnings. If you sell a U.S. residence and claim the Canadian principal residence exemption on the full amount of the gain, no credit will be given for any capital gains taxes paid in the United States.

It has become much more difficult in recent years to legally shelter income in a foreign jurisdiction. Generally, if you are earning investment income, such as dividends or interest (not capital gains) in a tax haven, you will be required to report it for Canadian tax purposes, no matter what the arrangement. Methods still abound for sheltering earnings outside Canada, but they tend be extremely complex, and often involve considerable expense. Of course, the ultimate solution is always available — leave Canada permanently. This is discussed in more detail in Chapter 17.

Most Canadians have enough trouble dealing with their own tax system. If you are trying deal with one or two others at the same time, you will undoubtedly benefit from professional advice. The unwary can fall into tax traps in the most unlikely places.

Chapter 11 — Estate Planning

If you don't put your house in order, who will? It's unlikely that your financial affairs will take care of themselves should you suddenly die. They will, though, if you begin planning now for your death and what will happen to your assets. Putting a well-thought-out estate plan into action will make the financial side of life much easier on your heirs when you die, especially your spouse. This is certainly the case if your spouse has not been heavily involved with your general financial planning up to this point. And a little planning now should produce big savings down the road, primarily tax savings, but also probably savings in the form of reduced professional fees. These savings will certainly be appreciated by your heirs and could make a big difference to how comfortable your spouse will end up should you die first.

Estate planning is nothing more than a relatively straightforward extension of your general financial planning. Your objectives when developing an estate plan are generally to:

- ensure that you and your family are provided for adequately now and during your retirement, and that your heirs are adequately provided for after your death;
- distribute your assets according to your wishes, both during your lifetime and after your death, while ensuring that the maximum benefits available accrue to your beneficiaries;
- minimize various forms of wealth erosion, taxes being the most prominent, both now and in the future.

Retirement planning shares two of these goals — providing adequately for you and your family and minimizing taxes. However, unless you are quite well off, your estate planning and retirement planning objectives may come into conflict. With estate planning, you are interested in passing on to your heirs as much of your accumulated wealth as possible. From a retirement planning perspective, you are interested in accumulating and retaining as much wealth as possible, which will be used to generate sufficient retirement income. Estate planning looks toward conserving assets and putting them into someone else's hands. Retirement planning focuses on keeping assets in your hands and, in many cases, eventually exhausting them. Concentrating on one type of planning to the exclusion of the other will likely lead to problems, some of which may be very difficult to rectify.

Attitudes today are changing. Those who have already retired tend to want to conserve their assets and pass them on to their children. However, their children, who are often better off than their parents, are much more willing to focus on themselves and wish their parents would do the same. We agree with the children. While basic estate planning certainly has its place in everyone's financial affairs, it ought to take a back seat to retirement planning. In other words, providing for yourself during retirement ought to be the objective of your financial plan as you approach retirement age. If you have considerable wealth, or you are convinced that your retirement needs are more than adequately provided for, then some serious estate planning may be in order. But bear in mind that estate planning involves giving up control and ownership of assets that you now own and which could be used to generate income during your retirement years. If your children own them, you may have to look elsewhere for income if you haven't provided for yourself properly.

As you approach retirement age, you will probably be giving some thought to the disposition of your assets on your and/or your spouse's death. The deemed disposition rules impose tax on unrealized capital gains at the time of your death, although this rule can be waived if assets are passing to your spouse or to a special trust for your spouse. He or she will eventually become subject to the deemed disposition rules. Nevertheless, the value of your assets could eventually be seriously eroded by these taxes. Carefully disposing of some of your assets during your lifetime can alleviate this future tax burden.

From a tax point of view, your estate planning goals generally are to:

- minimize and defer taxes now and in the future to preserve your accumulated wealth;
- shift any potential tax burden that may arise on a particular asset to your heirs so that the tax becomes payable only when your heirs eventually sell the asset;
- minimize taxes at death to maximize the amount of your accumulated wealth that passes to your intended heirs.

KEEPING YOUR WILL UP-TO-DATE

In your will, you appoint executors for your estate, name your beneficiaries, and provide for the distribution of your assets. It is important that you and your spouse draw up your wills together and agree on the objectives that you want to achieve under the terms in both your wills. Bear in mind that the family or succession law in most provinces contains regulations that ensure a spouse and dependent children will be adequately provided for on your death, no matter what your will might say. In most provinces, your spouse may be automatically entitled to half the "matrimonial" assets on your death, if there are no dependent children. Matrimonial assets generally include everything accumulated during the marriage, plus the matrimonial home, but exclude gifts and the value of most property brought into the marriage. The definition includes business assets in many provinces, but generally excludes assets excluded under a marriage contract.

Provincial law also governs what happens to your assets should you die without a will. In most cases, this will not coincide with how you had planned for your assets to be distributed.

PRACTICAL POINTER   It is vital that you appoint a competent and caring executor. The executor is charged with interpreting your wishes as expressed in your will and other documents, and carrying them out to the best of his or her ability. He or she is also charged with maintaining the value of your estate until all the assets are distributed.

Generally, you will want to empower the executor to make virtually all decisions concerning your estate that you had not anticipated. For example, if your executor feels that your business or investments would benefit from outside management until these assets are distributed, he or she should be so empowered.

You should mentally review your will once a year, and it should be given more thorough scrutiny once every five years at least. It should be revised immediately if the executor or one of your beneficiaries should die, of if there is any significant change in your family or financial situation. Do not forget to review and revise other parts of your estate and retirement plan, such as RRSPs, your pension plan and insurance policies, since beneficiary designations contained in these arrangements may need changing.

TAXES ON DEATH

There are no Canadian "death taxes" per se, or succession duties. However, all assets of an individual are deemed to be disposed of immediately prior to death. Thus, capital gains and losses, and recapture of previously claimed capital cost allowance (tax depreciation) will result from this deemed disposition. Of course, all income earned by the deceased up to the time of death is subject to tax. As might be expected, there are numerous exceptions to these general rules and a number of special cases.

Generally, gains and income are taxed in the hands of the deceased or the estate of the deceased before assets can be passed on to beneficiaries. If a trust is created under the will of the deceased, tax may be payable by the trust, or by beneficiaries of the trust.

The year an individual dies, his or her taxation year runs from January 1 to the date of death. A final return of income, the "terminal return", must be filed on behalf of the deceased. All income earned to the date of death, including amounts accrued but not yet received at the time of death and all capital gains and losses realized in the period, must be reported.

As well, the deceased is deemed to have disposed of all his or her capital property immediately before death. Non-depreciable capital property is deemed to be disposed of at its fair market value. Currently, the rules provide that depreciable property is deemed disposed of at a value midway between its undepreciated capital cost and its fair market value. It is proposed that the deemed disposition of any depreciable property on death after 1992 take place at fair market value. A deemed disposition of a resource property at death results in the inclusion of the full fair market value as income on the terminal return.

A deemed disposition for tax purposes, and the resulting tax, occurs even though there has been no actual disposition of the asset. If large capital gains have accrued on the asset, significant amounts of tax could be payable. The cash to pay this tax liability must be found from the rest of the estate; otherwise, the asset may have to be sold. The capital gains exemption is available in the year of death, but the alternative minimum tax (AMT) is not applicable.

The major exception to these deemed disposition rules occurs when the deceased's spouse inherits the assets. There is still a deemed disposition, but the spouse takes over the deceased's cost base of the assets. There are no capital gains, or in the case of depreciable property, no recapture of capital cost allowance. Only when the spouse eventually disposes of the property will tax on the gains or recapture arise. If the spouse inherits the family home, the principal residence designation of the deceased is transferred to the spouse (see Chapter 13). Thus, all accumulated gains remain tax-free when the house is eventually sold by the spouse. These same rules also apply if the assets go to a trust of which only the surviving spouse has access to the income and capital.

PRACTICAL POINTER   A spouse can elect for these "rollover" rules not to apply to specific assets or groups of assets. For example, if the deceased's $100,000 capital gains exemption is still available, or the deceased has accrued capital losses at the time of death, the surviving spouse should elect that certain property is deemed disposed of at fair market value to claim the exemption, or to use up the losses. The surviving spouse is then deemed to acquire the property at a cost equal to its fair market value, which should reduce the gain upon an eventual disposition. In this way, the remaining capital gains exemption or capital losses of the deceased are, in effect, transferred to the surviving spouse.

Farm property can also be bequeathed to a child, grandchild, or great-grandchild of the deceased on a tax-deferred basis, although since the $400,000 capital gains exemption is available for certain farm property, as well as the $100,000 exemption, it would be wise to elect a value for the farm property that fully utilizes the remaining exemption of the deceased.

Special rules also apply to RRSPs, RRIFs, and pension plans. If your spouse is the beneficiary of the plan or of your estate, he or she may become the annuitant of your RRSP or RRIF, or the amounts may be transferred into his or her RRSP with no tax consequences. The surviving spouse can also use the RRSP funds to buy an annuity or transfer the amount to his or her RRIF. If you have no spouse, amounts may be transferred to the RRSP of financially dependent children, or an annuity to age 18 may be purchased for younger children. If you die before your pension benefits start, your spouse may have the opportunity of receiving benefits from the plan, which will be reduced, since they will be received before normal retirement age. Your spouse also may transfer your accumulated benefits to his or her own RRSP on a tax-deferred basis.

A variety of tax planning opportunities may be available to the executor of your estate after you die. For example, depending on the circumstances, three other types of income tax returns can be filed in the year of death, which may reduce the deceased's tax burden and so provide more funds for the heirs. Or, if the estate of the deceased earns significant income before it is settled, the executor may opt to elect for income to be attributed to one or more preferred beneficiaries (usually a minor child), in which case the income is taxed in the beneficiary's hands, not in the estate. This would be advantageous only if the beneficiary were taxed at a lower rate than the estate.

PRACTICAL POINTER It is important that you empower your executor to undertake whatever testamentary tax planning may be necessary to reduce tax in your final return of income, and to reduce the impact that taxes will have on your estate and your intended beneficiaries.

If you own assets in another country, foreign death taxes may pose unexpected and sometimes serious tax and other financial problems. The problems associated with estate tax levied by the United States are discussed briefly in later chapters. Suffice it to say here, it is imperative that your executor and heirs obtain professional advice concerning these problems.

LIFE INSURANCE

Life insurance can be used for a variety of purposes in your estate planning program:

- as a tax-sheltered investment vehicle, if properly structured, for the accumulation of funds during your lifetime, with a tax-free payout arising upon your death;
- to provide a base for generating income to your surviving spouse should your pension and other retirement income arrangements not be sufficient;
- to provide cash upon death to cover taxes and other expenses, which would be particularly useful if valuable assets are bequeathed to children and it is impracticable to quickly sell the assets, such as an interest in a business, for a fair price;
- to help the surviving shareholders of a closely held company finance the purchase of shares from the estate or the heirs of a deceased shareholder;
- to provide additional assets to children who eventually are not to be involved in the family business or who will not be sharing in the distribution of valuable assets, for example, the family cottage.

Proceeds from almost all life insurance policies are not taxable in the hands of the beneficiary of the policy or the beneficiaries of the estate, should the insurance proceeds be payable to the estate.

The main drawback of life insurance is that it becomes prohibitively expensive as you get older — and, often, it just isn't necessary. Unless you have a good reason for buying it, the cost may outweigh any possible benefit. For instance, buying many types of life insurance to augment your estate which will eventually go to your children may not be a sound investment. The money that otherwise would go to pay the insurance premiums can be invested for your children or simply be used to augment your own retirement income. We reiterate our comments made earlier: your children probably would prefer that you and your spouse have a comfortable, secure and enjoyable retirement rather than scrimping and saving to provide a nest egg for them. After all, your children could be close to retirement age themselves when the two of you finally shuffle off this mortal coil.

There are essentially two types of life insurance policies: term insurance and whole life or permanent insurance. Term policies simply cover your life — they pay off should you die. Insurance companies offer a wide variety of term policies which include such options as a guarantee of insurability or steady premiums for life. Permanent insurance contains an investment aspect and the life insurance aspect. Premiums are generally much higher for permanent than for term insurance, but they remain at that level and finally end at a particular date, at which time your policy is paid up. After that time your policy continues to increase in value. You can cash in your permanent policy and receive a lump sum (it takes a few years for this to amount to much), or you can borrow against the policy. Generally, permanent policies are structured so as not to attract income tax on the investment aspect, although if you borrow against the policy or cash it in, tax may become payable.

ESTATE PLANNING TECHNIQUES

Most estate planning strategies obviously result in a benefit, but also involve a cost of some sort. The cost may be a loss or partial loss of control over a particular asset, loss of flexibility when planning the rest of your financial affairs, an immediate cost for professional fees and other expenses, and there may even be an immediate tax cost that is related to avoiding a much higher tax cost in the future.

GIFTING ASSETS

Most estate planning focuses on transferring the future growth in the value of an asset to your children, and so transferring any tax liability on future gains. The simplest way to effect this transfer is to gift the asset to the child. While this solves the future tax liability problem, there are at least three drawbacks to outright gifts.

First, you lose control over the asset. Since ownership is transferred to your child, the future income-earning potential of the asset is also transferred to the child.

Second, if the asset is transferred to a child under the age of 18, all income on the asset (but not capital gains) is attributed back to you and is taxed in your hands. However, any future capital gain will be realizable in the hands of your child, and attribution of income stops in the year the child turns 18. If the asset is transferred to your spouse, the attribution rules apply on all income and capital gains.

Third, when you gift the asset to your child, who can be any age, you are deemed to have disposed of the asset for proceeds equal to fair market value. Thus, any capital gain accrued up to that point must be recognized for tax purposes, even though you have not received any proceeds in respect of the gift. Still, the gain should be eligible for your $100,000 capital gains exemption.

The deemed disposition rules at fair market value do not apply on transfers to a spouse or when farm property is transferred to a child, grandchild, or great-grandchild. Generally, you should try to use up your exemption before using these rollover provisions, since they simply defer your tax liability to future years.

USING TRUSTS

A trust is nothing more than a method whereby one person holds property for the benefit of another person. A trust is created when a settlor transfers property to a trustee who holds the property for the benefit of a beneficiary. Trusts are either testamentary (arising on death) or *inter vivos* (arising during your lifetime).

In a typical situation, the settlor and trustee are one and the same — you — and the beneficiary would be your child or children. With a trust, you can transfer ownership of an asset to your children but retain control over the asset until it is distributed from the trust to your children. The transfer of the property to the trust must take place at fair market value if the children are beneficiaries. Thus, you must recognize any accrued capital gains for tax purposes at the time of transfer.

Income earned by the trust and left there is subject to tax. Most of the standard deductions and tax credits that can be used by individuals in the personal tax return are not available to trusts. An *inter vivos* trust is taxed at the top marginal rate. However, if income is directly distributed to beneficiaries or distributed by means of a preferred beneficiary election, the income is taxed in the hands of the beneficiaries. If they are your children, the rate of tax paid on the income may be considerably lower than that paid by you or paid by the trust. Such income retains its character when it is distributed. Thus Canadian dividends remain eligible for the dividend tax credit. Only three-quarters of capital gains are subject to tax and they remain eligible for the $100,000 capital gains exemption.

Under the preferred beneficiary election, income earned inside the trust is taxed in the hands of the beneficiaries, but it is not actually paid to them. The earnings remain in the trust to generate future earnings. A preferred beneficiary must be a Canadian resident and one of the following:

- the settlor of the trust, or his or her spouse or former spouse;
- a child, grandchild, or great-grandchild of the settlor;
- the spouse (but not former spouse) of a child, grandchild, or great-grandchild of the settlor.

As well, no one can contribute more assets to the trust than the settlor.

Special rules require a trust to dispose of its property for tax purposes every 21 years, which generally means that significant capital gains could arise. However, proposed legislation allows this 21-year rule to be waived if there is an "exempt beneficiary" under the trust. An exempt beneficiary is one who is alive and who is generally either the settlor of trust or related to the settlor or the settlor's spouse. Such relations include only a spouse or former spouse, a grandparent, parent, brother, sister, child, niece, or nephew.

ESTATE FREEZING

While trusts solve several problems, they do not solve the main one of retaining access to the future income-earning ability of the assets that you want to give to your children, and eliminating the deemed disposition and resulting capital gain problem. While this may seem like having your cake and eating it too, this dilemma can be partially or wholly solved relatively easily through an estate freeze.

Estate freezing can be defined in general terms as a method of organizing your affairs so as to permit any future appreciation in the value of selected assets to accrue to others, usually your children. With an estate freeze, you retain, or at least have access to, the current value of the frozen asset; only the future increases in value are transferred to the child. It is also possible for you to retain control over the assets.

Selling the asset to your child is the simplest of estate freezes. Usually the transferor parent is not interested in receiving the proceeds of the sale immediately, but he or she would like to keep the door open and may also want to receive some of the income from the assets, even though they now belong to the child. Typically, you would take back a note payable from the child as payment for the sale price of the asset. Thus, you have sold an asset likely to grow in value for one that has a fixed value.

You can either charge interest on the note or make it interest-free. Typically, such notes are payable on demand. If the asset is sold to a minor child and interest is not paid, the attribution rules will apply to any income earned on the asset. If you charge interest at commercial rates or the government's prescribed rate, the attribution rules will not apply to put the income back into your hands. By charging interest, you participate in the income-earning ability of the asset. By ensuring that the note is structured as a demand note secured by the asset, you retain a certain degree of control over the asset — you can always demand payment of the note in full, or in theory take back the asset. This kind of flexibility and protection is advisable as you get closer to retirement age if you are still not certain that you will have sufficient income to see you and your spouse through your retirement years. You can always forgive the note at a future date. In fact, this forgiveness should form part of your will, if that is your intent. Forgiving the loan while you are alive may have income tax implications for the debtor, so professional advice should be sought in this area.

While this strategy achieves a number of goals, you will still be deemed to have disposed of the asset at fair market value for tax purposes when you sell it to the child, even though you only take back a note payable. Partial relief is available under the reserve provisions in the Income Tax Act. Essentially, these say that you will be able to defer recognizing four-fifths of the gain in the year of transfer. You must recognize one-fifth in each of the succeeding four years so that the entire gain is subject to tax by the end of the fourth year after you sell the asset to your child. The reserve mechanism would be invoked only for that portion of any gain not covered by your lifetime $100,000 capital gains exemption.

Investment Corporation Freeze

The various corporate freezes discussed in the next chapter also apply if your investment assets are held by a corporation that you control. One of two methods would probably be used. You might consider a holding company freeze. Your children, who should all be over the age of 18, would incorporate the holding company and acquire the common shares for a nominal amount. You would then transfer your shares in the investment corporation to this holding company on a tax-deferred basis and take back voting preferred shares in the holding company as consideration for the transfer. These voting preferred shares would have a redemption value equal to the value of the common shares of the investment corporation that you transferred to the holding company. Receiving voting preferred shares would allow you to retain control over the assets (the shares of the investment corporation), still receive income from these assets if that is your wish, and defer the recognition of any accrued capital gains on the shares that you own in the investment corporation. To achieve this last point, you and the holding company must make the appropriate income tax election. If you want the cash from the sale, you can cause the holding company to retract your preference shares, which generally would have a value equal to the fair market value of the assets in your investment corporation at the time your shares were transferred to the holding company. Bear in mind that the attribution rules will apply if any of your children are under 18. Of course they cease to apply once your child turns 18.

You might also want to consider an "internal freeze" with your investment corporation. However, this may not be possible in all provinces and it may be a bit more complex. Bear in mind that both types of freezes involve some expense. You will definitely need professional advice and there will be a cost involved with setting up a new corporation or reorganizing an existing one. There will also be the ongoing costs of maintaining a new corporation or the old one.

If your investment assets are not incorporated, you should glance over the material in the preceding chapter. Generally, there is no tax advantage to incorporating an investment portfolio, but there can be definite income splitting and estate planning benefits to be found.

Chapter 12 — Estate and Succession Planning for the Owner-Manager

Planning for retirement, planning for your heirs upon your death, and planning for the person who takes over the reins of your business when you exit are inextricably tied up together; yet your planning objectives in each area may be in conflict. We discussed general estate planning in the previous chapter. This chapter deals only with estate planning in the context of succession planning for your business. Please note that estate and succession planning for your business are discussed in much greater detail in *Tax Planning for Success.*

Some owner-managers bow out of their businesses completely when they retire, selling all the stock they own, ensuring that all debt is repaid, and severing all management contact. Others stay involved with the business in one form or another for years after they retire, often until they die. This most often happens when family members or perhaps key employees take over the business on the owner-manager's retirement.

While this book focuses on retirement planning, you cannot ignore estate planning in your decision making. Of course, you are already planning for your family, primarily you and your spouse. In one of the early chapters, we stressed that your spouse should be involved in many of your determinations. It is just not practicable to undertake retirement planning for your business without considering the possibility of your early demise, either while you still own the business or when you are retired but still involved with it to some degree.

Turning your thoughts to estate and succession planning means asking some tough questions. We'll start off with a couple of easy ones.

- Have you made out a will? If you have, when was the last time you reviewed it? When was the last time you revised it?
- Have your personal circumstances changed since the last time you looked at your will? Have you divorced or have you remarried? Have you had more children? Have your children married?
- Has your spouse taken a greater interest in the business? Have you involved your children in the business? Are they ready to take over control of it should you die or become seriously disabled? What do other shareholders, if any, think of this?
- How has your business changed since the last time you reviewed your will and your insurance arrangements? Is it generating more income and profit? Have you taken on new partners who are shareholders? Have any key employees demonstrated a desire to take over the business once you bow out?
- What are the prospects for your business? Will it remain profitable until you retire? Are there likely to be a few bumpy patches along the way that could affect your ultimate retirement income?
- Have you given any thought to how you want to get retirement income out of your business? Do you plan to sell it? Do you want to stay involved? How do you want to stay involved? Do you want to retain an active managerial role? Or do you simply want an ownership role that generates retirement income?
- When was the last time you reviewed your insurance program? Should you suddenly die or suffer a serious disability, do you have a complete succession program in place? Has your business and its value changed substantially since you put those programs into place?
- If you have more than one child, have you figured out how to deal with each child fairly? If one gets the business, what assets do the other children get? How will your spouse be dealt with if one or more of your children get the business? Do you have substantial other assets? Will your spouse have to do with less income for a lengthy period if your children get the business?
- Have you discussed your retirement, estate, and succession planning with your spouse? Does he or she agree with your plans?

If there is disagreement, have you determined what the impact of the family law and laws of succession in your province may have on your business?

- Does your business currently qualify for the $400,000 small business capital gains exemption? If it doesn't and you suddenly die before the business is "untainted", do you realize the tax consequences? Can your heirs afford the tax consequences without seriously jeopardizing the business?
- If your family will not take over the business, are there willing buyers waiting in the wings who will offer a fair price? If the business, and therefore its value, depends primarily on you, are there any measures you can take to enhance its sale value?

We looked at estate planning from the personal perspective in the previous chapter. From the perspective of the owner-manager, the same three estate planning objectives exist:

- ensure that your business provides adequately for you and your family now and in the future, and that the business provides adequately for your heirs after your death;
- distribute your business assets according to your wishes while ensuring that the maximum benefits available accrue to your beneficiaries;
- minimize wealth erosion, primarily taxes, both now and in the future.

A number of concerns must be addressed when you undertake any succession planning:

- picking and grooming your successors;
- ensuring that you and your family continue to receive sufficient income as the successor takes over the business;
- ensuring that all family members are treated equitably;
- ensuring that family members can sell the business, should they take it over, at a good price if they prove unable to operate it successfully;
- ensuring that your business continues to run smoothly as you put your succession plan into action.

Three issues top the list of possible concerns you will have as you develop a succession plan:

- Who gets what?
- How much control over the operation of the business should you retain?
- Where does the funding for the purchase and for your retirement come from?

We will address these issues in the next few pages. First, a short lesson on how you and your business are taxed should you die or sell the business. Bear in mind that, for tax purposes, a transfer of ownership of your business to your children or spouse is essentially the same as selling it to an outside party at arm's length.

First, if you sell the shares in the business, which assumes that the business is incorporated, this is the same as selling any other shares in a corporation, with one major exception: you are entitled to the $400,000 small business capital gains exemption if your corporation qualifies. We discussed this exemption in Chapter 9.

Second, it is possible to sell just the assets of the business. However, you will not then be eligible for the $400,000 exemption, although steps can be taken to use this up before you sell. When selling assets, the vendor is liable for tax on capital gains, if the assets have increased in value, and recapture of capital cost allowance (CCA or tax depreciation) previously claimed, which is an income item and is taxed at normal rates. Sales tax issues will also arise.

Third, as explained in Chapter 11, you are deemed to have disposed of all your assets upon death, which means capital gains may arise. Assets include your business assets and any shares you own in a corporation. Tax can be deferred if the assets are bequeathed to your spouse or a trust for your spouse. However, if the assets go directly to your children, they must be transferred at fair market value and tax on any gains will have to be dealt with in your final tax return. The gains will be eligible for the $100,000 capital gains exemption and gains on the shares of your corporation will be eligible for the $400,000 exemption if the business qualifies.

Fourth, if you transfer ownership in your business to your children before or at the time you retire, the same rules for recognizing any inherent gains apply, even though you may be essentially giving the business to the child for nothing. The transfer or gift will be deemed to take place at fair market value and you must recognize any gains. However, if you actually sell the business to your children, which you are likely to do in order to generate retirement income, but do not receive the proceeds of the sale immediately, you can claim a tax "reserve" against proceeds not received. The reserve provisions in the tax law essentially say that you must report for tax purposes at least one-fifth of the capital gain in the year of sale and a further one-fifth in each of the succeeding four years so that by the fifth year the entire capital gain has become subject to tax. If you receive more than one-fifth of the proceeds in any particular year, a larger proportion of the capital gain must be brought into income for tax purposes. Note that there are no provisions for claiming a reserve against recaptured CCA. It must be recognized in its entirety in the year of sale.

Fifth, if you own a qualifying farm business, it may be transferred at any value between cost and fair market value to your children, grandchildren, or great grandchildren, either while you are alive or upon death. The $400,000 capital gains exemption as well as the general $100,000 exemption is available on capital gains arising on such transfers.

A variety of other tax provisions affects sales and transfers of your business to family members or to outside parties. For example, you may be caught by the attribution rules if you transfer shares or assets in your business to your spouse, as discussed above in Chapter 10. However, your spouse can acquire these shares or assets from you at fair market value with his or her own funds and the attribution rules will not apply. You can also lend funds to your spouse for the purchase, as long as your spouse pays interest on the loan at the prescribed interest rate set by the government.

You should also note that the tax law contains far-reaching general anti-avoidance rules (GAAR) that prohibit a variety of transactions that are undertaken for the sole purpose of reducing taxes and that may have no business reason.

WILLS AND INSURANCE PROTECTION

It goes without saying that you should have a will. It should be reviewed annually and probably it should have a professional review and updating every five years, or more often if your personal, financial, or business circumstances change.

An adequate, up-to-date insurance program is essential for every owner-manager. Taxes and other expenses at death can cripple a business. If your children take over the company, they may be left with inadequate working capital and debts that will make running the company difficult. Combine this with the fact that you are no longer at the helm, and the business can be permanently ruined. Cash from a life insurance settlement won't solve every problem that arises when you die, but it will smooth over many and give your business a much better chance of surviving your death.

In many cases, unless you have insurance, it is impossible to provide adequately for your spouse on your death while at the same time ensuring the continued viability of your business if your children will be taking it over. Typically, they will not have the cash to buy it outright from your estate or your surviving spouse, which otherwise would have provided your spouse with the necessary retirement income. If you do not have a proper insurance program in place, it may be necessary to sell the business to a third party, thereby depriving your children of the opportunity to own the business and run it themselves. If you have other partners or shareholders in your business, life insurance is vital to ensure that on the death of one partner, the others have the opportunity to buy the deceased's share of the business.

Disability insurance should also be considered. A surprising number of people in the work force will suffer some type of disability during their career which will keep them away from their jobs for longer than three months. Could your business survive your absence for as long as three months or perhaps a year or two? Do you have sufficient cash reserves and savings to get you and your family through this period? If your business fails, will you have the cash to start up all over again, assuming your failed business doesn't continue to drain your cash once you recover from your disability?

ESTATE PLANNING FOR YOUR BUSINESS

Chances are your business has appreciated significantly in value since you acquired it or started it up. As you get close to retiring, you are probably thinking that you would like to crystallize those gains to take advantage of the $400,000 small business capital gains exemption, and you would like to ensure that those gains are still there when you bow out of the business. If your gains are substantial, you would also like to minimize any future tax liability. You are probably also ready to begin handing over ownership and control of the business to your children, if this is one of the goals of your succession planning.

Generally, these objectives can be accomplished in one relatively straightforward series of transactions, called an estate freeze. As detailed in the previous chapter, estate freezing is possible with any type of capital asset. With business assets, more types of estate freezing techniques are at your disposal, although some of them come at a price — they may be costly to implement and they may add an unwanted degree of complexity to the financial side of your life.

CORPORATE FREEZES

A corporate estate freeze is generally undertaken if you expect continued future growth in the value of your company or if you want to use up your $400,000 capital gains exemption. The corporate freeze also facilitates handing the reins of the business over to your children, even though the value of the business currently is prohibitively high from their perspective. With the more popular types of corporate freezes, you retain control over the business while freezing the value of your common shares, letting future growth in the value of the company accrue to your children.

The two most common freeze techniques are the internal freeze and a freeze using a holding company. With the first type, the internal freeze, you would convert your common shares to voting preference shares, assuming this is permitted under company legislation governing your corporation. A new class of common shares is then created, which the children purchase with their own funds for a nominal amount. You retain control of the corporation through the voting preferred shares, while your children participate in the future growth of the company through the common shares.

PRACTICAL POINTER   You and your company can make an income tax election that causes the transaction to take place at an amount anywhere between your cost and the fair market value of the common shares.

This could allow you to use up your $400,000 exemption when you exchange your common shares for the new voting preference shares.

Despite the many benefits that result from an internal freeze, your money is still tied up in the company and therefore exposed to some risk.

With the holding company freeze, a separate corporation is established and all the common shares of the holding company are acquired by your children for a nominal value. You transfer your common shares in your operating company to this new holding company in exchange for sufficient voting preferred shares to allow you to retain control over the holding company and therefore the operating company. You can transfer your common shares to the holding company on a tax-deferred basis, or consider transferring them at fair market value if you are entitled to use your $400,000 capital gains exemption. Again, your funds remain tied up in the company.

You also might want to consider an asset freeze, under which assets are transferred to another company that your children own. In exchange for the transfer you take back voting preferred shares in the new company and retain control over the assets. This may allow a method of separating certain assets, such as real estate, from the operating business.

Finally, you can effect a partial freeze of your company by simply retaining some of the common shares. You might consider this if the prime purpose of the freeze is simply to use up your $400,000 exemption.

Every owner-manager should note that corporate estate freezes are complex transactions that require professional advice every step of the way. Not everything that you probably want to do is sanctioned by the law, but your professional advisor should be able to devise a plan that accommodates most of your wishes.

SUCCESSION PLANNING

Deciding what to do with your business when it comes time for you to depart may be the hardest business decision you are likely to face.

- Should you give it to all your children or to just one child?
- If just one child is getting the business, how do you adequately compensate the others both now and in the future?
- Should you simply gift it to them or sell it to them?
- If you sell the business to your children or child, how long do you wait to get your money out?
- How long do you retain control of the business, or how soon do you begin to relinquish control?
- When and how do you begin to wind down your management activities?
- How involved do you stay if you decide to keep a finger in the business for a while?
- Should you sell it to outside parties and get your cash out as quickly as possible?
- Should you retain an interest in the business even though you are no longer involved with the day-to-day management?
- How long should you retain an interest in the business by way of shares or debt if you are going to be dependent on the dividend or interest income during your retirement years?
- How do you minimize the risk of not being able to access funds in the company when you need these to supplement your retirement income?
- How do you reconcile leaving your business to your spouse, when your spouse has not taken the slightest interest in running it?
- How do you ensure that your spouse receives a fair price if he or she intends to sell the business shortly after your death?

You can probably come up with a dozen more questions once you start to think about the problem — and make no mistake, it is a problem. Many businesses have foundered because the owner-manager did not come up with a viable succession plan at the right time. Or, when the owner-manager did come up with one, it was not flexible enough to allow for the inevitable curves that will be thrown the owner-manager's way as he or she gradually relinquishes control of the business.

Many parents dream of seeing their children take over their business when they decide to retire. In the best of all possible worlds, each child expresses a burning interest for the business to succeed and all contribute equally to the success of the business. In reality, siblings don't often get along that spectacularly, or even well enough to run a profitable business for any length of time. They are usually of uneven abilities, at least as far as running a business is concerned, and their interest levels are also likely to be all over the map.

PRACTICAL POINTER   Truth be known, the easiest way to deal with your business on retirement is to sell it to an outside party. Depending on the buyer, you might be better off getting all your cash out immediately. Or, if the buyer is likely to add something positive to the business that will increase profits, you might want to stay involved through a minority ownership, holding debt, or a management contract.

Selling your business this cold-heartedly may go against the grain, especially if you have laboured for several decades to build it up and would prefer to retain some involvement during at least the first years of your retirement. Gradually turning your business over to one child, assuming the interest and ability is there, may be the most appropriate course of action. This, of course, also assumes that you can afford to leave your investment in the corporation until your child is able to begin to buy you out for cash. Several of the freezing techniques dovetail nicely with this type of succession planning.

For example, let's assume that one of your children has expressed an interest in taking over your business. Using either the internal freeze or the holding company reorganization, your child would end up owning the common shares and participate in the future growth in the value of the company, while you would retain control over the corporation through your voting preferred shares. As your child gradually gains experience and begins to manage the business on a day-to-day basis, you might begin to have the corporation redeem, that is, buy back, some of your preferred shares. Eventually, your child would have sufficient common shares to exercise control over the company, while you would have received much of your investment out of the corporation which would be put toward supplementing your retirement income. If you did not need the cash immediately, you could lend it back to the corporation on whatever terms seemed appropriate.

The major drawback to this type of plan is that your funds, which you may have been counting on to generate the bulk of your retirement income, remain tied up in the company until you begin the share redemption process. If the company does not prove to be as profitable as you expected with your child running it, or the business experiences cash flow problems, you may have trouble getting your cash out when you want it. In the extreme case, you may have misjudged your child completely, and once he or she becomes involved, your business may begin a slow downward spiral.

PRACTICAL POINTER   **You can partially protect yourself against these possibilities by transferring valuable assets out of your corporation and leasing them back to the company. Should the company falter, you still own these assets and can sell them to generate retirement income.**

Of course, if you have other children, that still leaves the problem of how to treat them fairly. Yes, the one child may eventually pay you the fair market value for your interest in the business at the time it was frozen. But you gave that child the opportunity to participate in the future growth of the company, which was not given to the other children, and that child also, in effect, received an interest-free loan from you until your preferred shares were redeemed, unless you were receiving dividends on your shares every year at market rates. This is a problem that you may not be able to solve immediately, especially if your company is your largest asset and you have no other liquid assets readily available to, for instance, help the other children acquire their first home.

The problem may be eventually solved on your and your spouse's death, when all your children finally come into their inheritance. Unfortunately, there still may not be enough available to treat each child equitably. One solution is to allow each child to participate in the growth and income of the corporation while leaving one child definitely in control of the company. While not a perfect solution, it may be the only one open to you if life insurance has become prohibitively expensive.

PLANNING YOUR RETIREMENT INCOME

As we noted at the beginning of this chapter, it is not wise to undertake estate and succession planning without taking into consideration your retirement needs. For many owner-managers, the investment in their business will generate the bulk of their retirement income. That investment must be turned into a steady stream of income in some manner at or after retirement. Prudent planners will want to expose that potential income to as little risk as possible. After all, if you bow out of your business at age 60, you and your spouse may very well need that income stream to keep flowing for at least the next 30 years, and maybe longer. Currently, one-third of all people who reach age 71 make it past age 90.

Dividends

In passing, we noted that you may be receiving income from your investment in the business in a variety of ways. Chances are that you will receive dividends on shares you still own in your company. These may be common or preferred shares. You may have a variety of agreements attached to the payment of dividends on the shares. For example, dividends may be paid at a fixed rate on the preferred shares and must be paid in full before any dividends are paid on the common shares.

No matter what type of agreements you have made, your income from these shares is still at considerable risk if you no longer control the company or are not actively involved in its management. This risk factor generally increases, the further removed you are from the company in terms of control, management, and length of time you have been retired. This is why many owner-managers also institute a share retraction arrangement when they establish preferred shares, or a buy-out arrangement for any shares they still own when they finally relinquish control of their companies. Making the shares retractable gives the owner-manager the ability to force the company to buy back or redeem his or her shares.

Despite the risk factor, receiving income from your shares in your old company has two major attractions. First is the flexibility. You can design the shares in almost any manner you desire and, while you still have control of the company, provide for dividend payments that meet your specific income needs. A retraction or buy-out arrangement increases the flexibility. Second, the dividend rate could be much higher than you could otherwise achieve if you invested your funds conventionally. If your business remains profitable, your income should be greatly enhanced, assuming that is the type of deal you arrange when you sell or transfer ownership of your business.

Interest

Your investment in your business could produce interest income in a number of different ways.

- You may have lent the corporation money in the past, and either just interest or principal plus interest is to be paid to you during retirement.
- When you sell the business, part of the proceeds paid to you by the purchaser may be in the form of debt that pays interest and is repayable during retirement.
- When you transfer the business to your children, you may take back a note from them, which may be interest-bearing and on which you may demand eventual repayment.

In any of these cases, your funds remain at considerable risk because the payment of interest and the eventual repayment of the debt may depend to a great extent on the future health of your old business.

PRACTICAL POINTER   The arrangements you make with respect to the debt could lessen the risk substantially. For example, debt owed by the corporation could be secured by all or some of the fixed assets of the company. Interest payments on your corporate debt could be required to be paid before interest is paid on any other debt, or dividends are paid on shares. Debt held personally could take the form of a mortgage on the new shareholder's home. Any debt or notes payable could be payable on demand, so that, if the company looked like it was getting into trouble, you could step in and salvage much of what was owed to you.

Debt has one major advantage over dividends, namely, that dividend payments are generally subordinate to interest payments on debt and therefore are less risky. Of course, with a prosperous company, the dividend payments could be much larger and there may be the possibility of appreciation in the value of the shares that you still hold.

Leasing Income

Many owner-managers transfer certain assets out of their operating company before they retire and rely on them as a secure source of retirement income. For example, if your company owns a valuable building, or equipment that has an extremely long life, you could, on a tax-deferred basis, spin it into another corporation that you own and then charge the operating company rent for the building or equipment. When you retired and sold the business, you would enter into a long-term agreement with your old company for leasing the assets.

This arrangement has a number of advantages:

- It reduces the value of the operating company when it comes time to transfer it to your children or sell it to outside parties. This generally would make a transfer easier, since the child would not have to come up with as much cash to take control of the company. It would also facilitate a sale if the buyer is hesitant about paying cash up front.
- By taking the valuable assets out of the operating company before you sell it or transfer control, you have reduced your risk considerably. The value of your investment no longer depends entirely on the health of your old company, although this may not be the case if the asset transferred is special equipment that has significant value only to the operating company. Depending on the nature of the asset, you may be able to sell it or lease it to another business should your old company fail.
- You may gain a significant degree of inflation protection setting up such a new leasing company. The lease payments may increase over time, assuming that the value of the assets is maintained or increases. If the value of the assets increases, which is likely if real estate is spun out of the operating company, you have the potential of sitting on a large capital gain a few years down the road. If you decide to liquidate the assets, the proceeds can be used to generate retirement income.
- Since your retirement income is being generated in the leasing corporation, you have more opportunity to defer income if you don't need it immediately during the early years of your retirement, or you may even be able to generate extra income by having the leasing corporation pay you a salary for your management activities.

The major disadvantage of this type of arrangement is that you have set up a retirement business that will need taking care of, although if you lose interest, it can probably be managed by an outside party. Or you could simply sell the assets and wind up the company.

The transfer of assets from one corporation to another, especially if a sale to an arm's-length party may be contemplated, is a fairly complex area. Professional advice should be sought so that you do not end up with a large tax liability when you least expect it.

Income from Lump-Sum Proceeds

Chances are that at some point you will receive fairly large lump sums of money as a result of selling your business or turning it over to your children. Your objective will be to arrange for as much as possible of the sale proceeds to be eligible for your and your spouse's $400,000 small business capital gains exemptions. Unfortunately, any gains in excess of those covered by the exemptions will be taxed immediately with little opportunity to defer tax on the excess gain by way of a deferred income plan. They cannot simply be transferred to an RRSP or RRIF.

PRACTICAL POINTER   Consider arranging for your corporation to pay you a retiring allowance when you leave the business. A retiring allowance includes any amount received by you upon your retirement from the corporation that previously employed you. Up to $2,000 for each year you were an employee of the corporation, plus an additional $1,500 for each year before 1989 that you were employed and not a member of a registered pension plan, may be transferred directly to your RRSP. As a result, tax will be deferred until you withdraw it in the form of retirement income (see Chapter 5 for more on retiring allowances).

This strategy should be compared with the financial advantage of receiving the amount as a capital gain resulting from the sale of your business. The tax on the capital gain will be approximately three-quarters of the tax you eventually pay on the retiring allowance. However, the amount transferred to your RRSP earns income which is tax-sheltered as long as it stays in your RRSP. Interest and dividends earned on the proceeds from the sale of your business will not be sheltered. Generally, you will have to retain the amount in your RRSP or RRIF for a few years before it will be worthwhile taking the retirement allowance route. Since only minimum amounts must be withdrawn from an RRIF each year, this should not pose a problem.

Earnout on a Sale of the Business

Structuring the sale of your business based partially on an earnout arrangement can be risky, but also may net you considerably more than if you received all the proceeds of the sale up front. If you retire at the time the business is sold, the earnout payments will form part of your retirement income.

Earnouts are often favoured by both buyer and seller. The seller hopes to get more cash from the sale than he or she otherwise would have. Many owner-managers see the earnout arrangement as a way of keeping their finger in the business for a while longer, but on a reduced level of activity. Buyers prefer them for a variety of reasons. Less cash must be made available up front for the purchase. If the business isn't as profitable as expected, the buyer may end up paying less than if all the cash had been advanced up front. But primarily, an earnout arrangement tends to ensure that the former owner will use his or her best efforts to maintain the profitability of the business, since this is in everyone's best interests.

As the seller of a business, your prime risk is that the fortunes of the business will decline once it is sold, no matter what you do to ensure that the business remains healthy. You also run the risk that during the earnout period, you may experience health problems or even die, which will seriously impair earnout payments to you, your spouse, or your heirs. This concern must be balanced against the possibility of receiving considerably more for your business than you would otherwise expect to receive.

Management Agreements

If you sell your company or transfer it to your children, you may agree to stay on for a few years in a management capacity, but perhaps with reduced duties. Again, this is common in situations where the owner-manager is vital to profitability and his or her continued presence for a period of time is necessary to ensure the viability of the business.

You should definitely specify a description of your duties and the remuneration you are to receive in the contract. The terms might also provide that you are to be paid on the same *pro rata* basis as the new owners and your remuneration must be paid before any dividends are paid to the new owners.

Chapter 13 — Planning for Your Principal Residence

When it comes to getting ready for retirement, there's no place like an owner-occupied home. If you are like most Canadians, your home is your most valuable asset, and the value that you have accumulated in your home gives you a great deal of flexibility when it comes to planning the financial aspects of your retirement.

- Your home can provide a significant degree of inflation protection.
- Your home gets you out of the rental rate spiral that traps so many seniors.
- Later on in your retirement years, your home can provide a source of income if necessary.
- When ownership finally becomes too much for you, if it ever does, your home opens up a number of options that may not otherwise have been available.
- If you decide to relocate in Canada or abroad, the equity you have built up in your home makes it easier to find new accommodation.
- Your home can actually be used to make travel much cheaper and more enjoyable.
- An owner-occupied home is one of the best tax shelters available.

Perhaps most importantly, a home is a valuable appreciating asset that you actually get to use and enjoy. There are few assets that are as safe and secure that can make that claim.

YOUR HOME AS AN INFLATION PROTECTOR

We discussed inflation earlier in Chapters 2 and 4. We just mention it briefly again. Inflation-protected company pensions are still rare, unless you happen to work for the government. You can build in a degree of inflation protection with your other assets, but it comes at a cost. With an RRSP, you have to accept smaller retirement income payments initially to achieve a reasonable degree of inflation protection.

A debt-free owner-occupied home, and even a mortgaged home, automatically provides you with a large degree of inflation protection. First, if you didn't own, you would be renting. Rents may go up every year and are subject to inflationary pressures just as any other commodity. If you have a mortgage, your payments remain constant unless interest rates change. Your payments may go up or down, but they never continually go up the way rents do.

Second, a well-maintained home that you have "got just the way you want" is relatively inexpensive to keep up year after year. Yes, there will be routine maintenance expenses, and after a while you may want to hire a gardener and someone to shovel the walks, but you have a great deal of control over these expenses, whereas rental rates are entirely out of your control.

Third, unfortunately you are subject to the same increases for utilities and property taxes that a renter likely must face. But in terms of the size of your investment, these make up only a small percentage and are usually manageable. In many areas, tax breaks are available for seniors on property taxes and other expenses of ownership. These tax breaks may be available if you rent, but, in some instances, they are not as generous.

Fourth, since you own your home, you are the one enjoying the increase in value, not a landlord. Depending on where you live, house prices have increased anywhere from 1 or 2 per cent to more than 10 per cent annually over the past few decades. Even if your home increases in value at a low rate, you are likely being protected from rental increases should you decide to eventually sell your home and move into rental accommodation.

This last point highlights a mistake many Canadians have made and lived to regret. Many sold their homes in the early 1980s and

moved to relatively luxurious, maintenance-free rental accommodation. As rental rates moved inexorably upward, they had to find
less and less expensive shelter. By the early 1990s it was impossible
for them to get back into the housing market and they could no
longer afford the type of accommodation they wanted. Unfortunately,
there was and still is no solution to their problem.

FINANCIAL FLEXIBILITY AND YOUR HOME

A debt-free home gives you an amazing amount of flexibility once
you retire. Most notably, all those dollars you were pouring into
the mortgage are freed up for other living expenses. This should
give your retirement a significant boost. This amount of financial
flexibility is simply not available if you rent. You have no choice
but to be paying something for shelter each month.

We cannot stress too strongly the importance of paying off your
mortgage before you retire. We mentioned in Chapter 8 that the
closer you get to retiring, the more sense it makes to devote all
your investment activity to paying off your mortgage if you still
have one. This means forgoing RRSP contributions, although ideally
you would like to both maximize your RRSP contributions and
pay off your mortgage.

If you find that your retirement income has become inadequate,
you might want to consider a reverse mortgage on your home. These
are structured in two different ways. The first is structured as a
life annuity on your life or the lives of both you and your spouse.
The lender assesses the value of your house and arranges for a life
annuity to be paid to you. The payments from the annuity and
the interest on the accumulated amount paid to you are registered
as an accumulating mortgage on your home. When you or your
surviving spouse dies, the house is sold and the mortgage is paid
off before amounts are distributed to any of your beneficiaries.
Monthly payments from the annuity are relatively low, considering
the value of your home, but with today's lower interest rates, payments have increased somewhat.

The second type, offered by credit unions and other financial
institutions, is structured as a line of credit. You are given a line

of credit based on the value of your home and the line of credit is secured by a mortgage on your home. You draw funds from the line of credit and interest is added to the amount borrowed. The maximum amount that you can borrow on the line of credit is adjusted as your home increases in value. You have the option of not making any payments on the line of credit, or you can make payments and reduce your outstanding balance.

Note that payments from a reverse mortgage are not taxable. Thus, if you are in the 40 per cent tax bracket and are receiving a $300-a-month payment on a reverse mortgage, it is roughly the same as receiving $500 a month from your pension plan or RRSP.

With both types of reverse mortgages, you can sell your home at any time. With the annuity, a calculation is performed and the mortgage balance is repaid to the issuer. Payments on the annuity cease. With the line-of-credit variety, you simply pay off the outstanding balance with the proceeds from the sale.

Nevertheless, both types of borrowing should be viewed as last-resort measures. However, in most cases, you will be better off using a reverse mortgage than selling your home and moving into rental accommodation, if you continue to own and live in your home for a number of years. You might want to get professional advice to confirm the numbers that are provided by the issuer of the reverse mortgage.

YOUR HOME AS AN OLD AGE PROTECTOR

While many Canadians manage to live in their homes their whole lives, many eventually have little choice but to move into other accommodation. The first step may be simply moving into a condominium or rental accommodation. But many end up in retirement homes with a greater or lesser degree of care. At this point, the value that has accumulated in your home becomes extremely important. Being able to count on several hundred thousand dollars from the sale of your home means that you have a great deal of control over the type of home you will be living in and the quality of care you will receive.

YOUR HOME AS RELOCATION INSURANCE

The cost of housing in Canada is relatively high compared with that in most other countries in the world, and there is a great disparity in the cost of housing among centres in Canada. If you happen to own a home in the Toronto, Vancouver, or Ottawa area, you will likely have built up enough equity in the home to enable you to move to any other area in the country, buy a comparable house, and in most cases have a considerable amount of money left over. Similarly, if you own a home in Calgary or Edmonton, or in most other southern Ontario centres, you will easily be able to buy into any market in Canada, except the most expensive ones. Those who don't live in these markets may have less flexibility if and when they decide to relocate, but still, housing is generally cheaper in the country than in the city and cheaper in smaller towns than big cities.

If you are relocating to another country, you may notice a similar advantage. Home prices in the United States are less expensive in most areas than home prices in Canada's major centres, and, if you are planning a move to a different country, you should, in many instances, have no trouble finding comparable accommodation for the same money.

Without a home, you may have more trouble entering the home ownership market in another country, unless you have a significant amount of funds accumulated and you are not relying on the investment income generated from these funds to finance a portion of your retirement expenses.

TRAVEL AND HOME SWAPPING

While not for everyone, many Canadians have discovered the joys, the convenience, the security, and the savings that ensue when you swap homes with another home owner in another area of Canada or another country. You can either make the arrangements yourself through newspaper advertisements, or use one of the services that put potential home swappers together. Two of the services operating in Canada have worldwide connections and have been getting home owners together for several decades. It is a simple matter of writing prospective swappers and arranging times. By using one of the services, you gain access to thousands of possible homes to trade.

There are two primary advantages to swapping homes:

- *Security* — In theory and in practice, the "do unto someone's home as you would have them do unto yours" aphorism holds true. Swapping is not the same as renting. You end up with a house sitter for your home while you are away (plant waterer, lawn mower, etc.) and, hopefully, the house sitter will care as much about your home as you do. Of course, you are on the other end, caring as much about the other person's home. For extended vacations, swapping may even help with your home insurance, which often contains clauses that prohibit extended vacancies.
- *Cost of travel* — By swapping homes, you are obviously going to save on accommodation and perhaps food if you do a lot of your cooking in the house. You may also save on travel expense if the home comes with a car. More importantly, you may get to travel to cities that you normally could not afford to visit for any length of time.

YOUR HOME AS A TAX SHELTER

Most Canadians have at one time or another taken advantage of the tax shelter aspects of their owner-occupied home. Whenever you have sold one home and bought another, you probably have not paid any tax on the gain realized on the sale of the old home. The principal residence exemption has taken care of any capital gains tax that otherwise would have been payable.

If you own only one home, the principal residence exemption rules are relatively straightforward. However, many Canadians approaching retirement have two homes, or a home in another country. They are also getting to the point where they may sell one or both homes, or are ready to buy one in another locality. It is essential that you are aware of the tax rules governing the sale of owner-occupied homes. You don't always automatically get the exemption. In fact, the principal residence exemption has not been available on second homes since 1982, and the $100,000 capital gains exemption on second homes is being phased out for homes owned before March 1992 and has been eliminated for homes purchased after February 1992. The phase-out of the $100,000 capital gains exemption and some planning possibilities are discussed in detail in the next chapter.

Principal Residence Exemption

Before 1972, capital gains were not taxed, which, of course, meant that gains on owner-occupied homes were also not taxed. Homes retained their tax-exempt status when the capital gains tax was introduced in 1972, and until the end of 1981, every individual was entitled to a tax exemption on his or her own owner-occupied home. Thus, if a couple owned both a city and a vacation home and they inhabited each home at some time during the year of ownership, they were entitled to a full exemption on the gains arising on both homes.

An owner-occupied home is defined as including a house, condominium, mobile home, trailer, houseboat, seasonal home, or share in a co-operative housing corporation. The home can be owned individually or with one or more other persons. A qualifying home does not have to be located in Canada. Thus, a Florida or Arizona condominium qualifies for the exemption. The owner or a family member must normally inhabit the home, which includes occasional residency in a vacation property.

Beginning in 1982, the rules were changed to allow "family units" an exemption on only one owner-occupied home. A family unit generally consists of a husband, wife, and all unmarried children under the age of 18. However, the exemption on a second home is still allowed for gains accrued up to the end of 1981. A portion of the gain accruing after 1981 may be eligible for your $100,000 capital gains exemption.

To find the exempt portion of your gain on a sale or deemed sale of your home for tax purposes (a deemed sale would, for instance, occur upon death if the home is going to a beneficiary other than your spouse), use the following formula:

$$\frac{1 + \text{Number of calendar years property is designated as a principal residence}}{\text{Number of years property is owned after 1971}} \times \text{Gain}$$

The plus 1 in the formula makes allowance for years when you sell a house and then buy another one in the same calendar year. Note that claiming a principal residence exemption does not interfere with your ability to claim the $100,000 capital gains exemption. To claim either exemption, you must be a Canadian resident. In the case of the principal residence exemption, you must be a Canadian resident in each year you designate the home to be your principal residence.

Beginning in 1993, common-law couples will be treated the same as married couples for purposes of claiming the principal residence exemption. Therefore, only one home can be designated as a principal residence for a particular calendar year after 1992 by common-law couples. Until the end of 1992, both members of a common-law couple could claim their own exemption on a home they own. It appears that gains accrued to the end of 1992 on both homes will still be exempt, although at the time this book went to press, legislation relating to the proposed change in the law had not been enacted.

It is important to note that gains accrued on a home you owned before the date you got married are eligible for your principal residence exemption and are not subject to the family unit rule.

Two Homes Owned

If you acquired two homes before 1982 that you still own today and each one otherwise qualifies for your principal residence exemption, a portion of the gain on the second home should be eligible for your principal residence exemption. However, you may have to rearrange the ownership of the home to ensure the maximum tax benefits. If the second home was acquired after 1981, and you sell one or both homes, your decision comes down to which home gets the principal residence exemption and which home you want to claim under your $100,000 capital gains exemption. No matter how you arrange your affairs, a portion of the gain on one home will be subject to some tax since the $100,000 exemption is being phased out for property sold after February 1992, although if you have capital losses available you may be able to eliminate all or a portion of the taxable gain. Deciding which home to claim under which exemption is discussed in Chapter 14.

If you are claiming the principal residence exemption on two homes since both were owned before 1982, careful consideration must be given to how the two homes are owned. Since you and your spouse each want to claim the exemption on one home, you should each own 100 per cent of one of the homes to maximize your claim. This is not the most common arrangement, however. If you jointly own the homes, you are each entitled to the exemption on only your share of the ownership in one home. This means that a portion of the gain could be exposed to tax.

PRACTICAL POINTER   Revenue Canada allows you to switch ownership of the homes before the sale and claim the exemption as if you were each a sole owner of one of the homes since the date of purchase. If one of the homes is jointly owned, and the other solely owned, the same result can be achieved by switching ownership on the jointly owned home.

The worst position to be in is if one spouse owns both homes outright. That spouse can claim the principal residence exemption on only one home. Revenue Canada allows a switch to sole or joint ownership before the sale. As a result, ownership of one home will be considered to be sole or joint since the purchase date, but the transferring spouse must also transfer his or her principal residence designation to the other spouse for any years that spouse wants to claim under the exemption formula. This puts the couple almost back where they were when the homes were owned by one spouse. However, with the transfer, both spouses can take advantage of the "plus 1" in the exemption formula, which provides a bit of relief from any tax that may be payable.

If both spouses have their $100,000 capital gains exemption available, you may be able to combine this exemption and the principal residence exemption on the sale of both homes and eliminate most of the potential tax. Bear in mind that you can designate any number of years under your principal residence exemption. The technique works no matter how the homes are owned before the sale.

For example, after switching ownership, assume that the husband owns the city home outright, and the wife owns the vacation house either outright or jointly with the husband. Both homes have been owned since 1972 and are being sold in 1993. If the husband claims the entire principal residence exemption on the city home, the wife will be able to protect the gain on the vacation home for only 11 out of 22 years from tax (1972 to 1981 plus one year). If the gain remaining after she claims her principal residence exemption exceeds $100,000, a significant amount of tax could be payable.

However, if the husband claims for only six of the years after 1981 (for instance, 1982 to 1987) the wife will also be able to claim for six years (1988 to 1993). Now only five years or 5/22 of the gain (22 years of ownership, 1972 to 1993) are exposed to tax in the hands of each spouse. If each have their $100,000 capital gains exemption available, a significant tax reduction should be obtainable, although with the phase-out rules for the exemption in effect, a portion of the gain will still be taxable.

There are two methods for determining a pre-1982 exempt gain. You can simply designate the particular years in the formula, or you are permitted to obtain a valuation of the property as at December 31, 1981, and then calculate the gain to the date of sale based on this valuation. The gain accrued to the end of 1981 will be exempt under the principal residence exemption rules. Getting such a valuation may be difficult and expensive, but possibly worthwhile. Be sure to get a qualified valuation, otherwise Revenue Canada may disallow your 1981 value.

If a portion of your gain on the sale is taxable, you should be aware of how the attribution rules will affect you (see Chapter 10 for a detailed explanation of these rules). If your spouse is the one claiming the taxable gain, and he or she has not contributed to the purchase of the home, the gain may be attributed back to you.

Chapter 14 — Second Property Strategies

PHASE-OUT OF THE $100,000 CAPITAL GAINS EXEMPTION

The proposed phase-out of the $100,000 capital gains exemption for real estate, which took effect on March 1, 1992, came as a shock to many Canadians who were getting ready to retire. We are a country of two-property owners, land being plentiful and, until recently, inexpensive. Many people approaching retirement age own a cottage, a ski chalet, or other type of recreational property. Many own rental properties that they are counting on to provide funding for their retirement years, and thousands own property in the southern United States or other sunbelt areas that they plan to use extensively during the winter months of their retirement.

Most two-property owners have made plans to eventually use their second properties in a variety of ways.

- Some have made plans to sell their city home and buy a southern United States property, while continuing to use the cottage in Canada during the spring, summer, and fall months.
- Some are thinking of eventually selling their city home and buying a condominium, getting rid of the upkeep and the maintenance, in favour of convenience.
- Many couples expect that they will sell their large city home, which is now too big for just the two of them, and find something a bit smaller.
- At the same time, many are probably thinking of looking for a larger recreational property, since the kids are now having their own kids, and vacations are getting a bit cramped.

- Some are considering buying a better-located cottage that has more amenities and is winterized so they can get more use out of it in their increased spare time once they retire.
- Potential Canadian snowbirds are thinking about upgrading their southern U.S. accommodation in anticipation of longer stays in the sunny south during the winter months.
- Most retirees have not lost sight of the possibility of eventually selling one of their properties to provide additional retirement funding if that ever becomes necessary.

All these people approaching retirement have one thing in common. They were counting on being able to use their principal residence exemptions and their $100,000 capital gains exemptions to their best advantage as they juggled their housing situation before or during their retirement years. They figured that when it came time to sell one or both properties, they would be protected from any taxable gains and be able to make the switches they were contemplating on a mostly, if not entirely, tax-free basis.

Beginning March 1, 1992, that is no longer the case. If you own two properties, you owe it to yourself and your family to familiarize yourself with the phase-out rules for the $100,000 capital gains exemption, and determine if there are any defensive strategies you can undertake now to save yourself, and possibly your family, a king-size headache sometime in the future. Please note that at the time this book went to press, the phase-out rules had not been enacted into law.

PROPERTY AFFECTED BY THE PHASE-OUT

All real estate affected by the phase-out of the $100,000 capital gains exemption is referred to as non-qualifying property. This can include homes, recreational properties, vacant land, rental properties, and farms. If these last two are operated as an active business, that is, they are not considered for tax purposes to be investment properties or personal property, they escape the new rules. Also affected are the shares of the capital stock of a corporation and an interest in a partnership or trust if the fair market value of the shares or interest is derived principally from real estate, again if no active business exists.

HOW THE PHASE-OUT WORKS

There are two major elements to the phase-out. First, the $100,000 capital gains exemption is simply eliminated for all non-qualifying property purchased after the end of February 1992. The principal residence exemption still remains, however, so at least the gain on one of your properties can still escape taxation on a sale no matter when it was purchased.

Second, for properties owned at the end of February 1992, the $100,000 exemption is being phased out. The phase-out formula is quite straightforward, although it could provide unfair results in some cases. Essentially it divides the time of ownership between the period when you were eligible for the exemption before March 1992 and the period when you were not eligible after February 1992. First, you calculate your gain on a sale of any non-qualifying property. Next, you determine the amount of the $100,000 exemption to which you are still entitled. Then you determine how much of the exemption you can claim on the gain on the sale of this non-qualifying property. The formula for doing so is simple — divide the number of months that you owned the property before March 1992 by the number of months of total ownership since the later of the date of acquisition and January 1, 1972. Multiply this fraction by your capital gain on the non-qualifying property to find out how much of the exemption you can actually claim. Note that any disallowed portion of the exemption is still eligible to be claimed on other capital gains, for instance, on a sale of stocks or bonds.

For example, assume that you have owned a cottage since September 1983 and you sell it in July 1993. Your total ownership adds up to 119 months. You owned the cottage for 102 months before March 1992, so the fraction of the capital gain that you can offset with the capital gains exemption is 102/119. If you calculated your eligible gain at $68,000, effectively you will be able to claim only $58,286 under your $100,000 capital gains exemption. Of the remaining $9,714, three-quarters, or $7,285, must be included in income where it is taxed at your regular rates. If you are in the top tax bracket, you could pay tax of over $3,600 on a transaction that you at one time thought would be tax-free.

The closer your purchase was to March 1992, the more seriously you will be affected by the phase-out. For example, if you had bought the cottage in September 1991 and sold it in July 1993 for a gain of $68,000, only 6/23 of the gain would be exempt, or $17,739. That would leave a gain of $50,261 exposed, of which three-quarters, or $37,696, would be taxable.

However, if you purchased your cottage before 1972, very little of your gain would be taxable. The fraction that remains eligible for your $100,000 capital gains exemption is 242/259, which means you effectively claim $63,537 under your exemption. Only $4,463 remains exposed.

WHO IS AFFECTED?

Of course you are affected by the phase-out only if you actually sell your real estate or are deemed to have sold it for tax purposes at fair market value. If you realize a loss or no gain, the phase-out certainly won't affect you. This may indeed be the case with many home owners who, in some markets, bought at the real estate peak in the late 1980s, only to watch in despair as real estate values plummeted over the next three or four years. Values in many cities have not yet caught up to those peaks and are not expected to for many years to come.

If you have quite a large gain on your property, you may also not be affected. Using the example above, let's change the gain to $140,000. If the property were purchased in September 1983, 102/119 of the gain, or $120,000, would qualify. Since the exemption is capped at $100,000, you would get to use your entire exemption and $40,000 of the gain would remain subject to tax. If you work through the numbers, you will see that the same situation would apply if you had owned the home since before 1972.

Again, let's assume that the gain is $140,000. Your exemption will not be cut into until July 1995 if you bought the property in 1983, or in March 2000 if the cottage was acquired before 1972. What this means is that if your gains are substantial and your property continues to increase in value each year, it may take a considerable number of years before the phase-out actually catches up to you and you are no longer able to claim the full $100,000 exemption, assuming that you even have that much available in a few years time.

A FEW BASICS TO BEAR IN MIND

First, it is important to remember that the principal residence exemption is not affected in any way by the phase-out of the $100,000 capital gains exemption for real estate. As explained in the previous chapter, you, or your family, are still eligible for a principal residence exemption on one property. Gains on other properties owned since before 1982 by other members of the "family unit" may also be partially offset by a principal residence exemption. Assuming that each of the properties qualifies as a principal residence, you can claim the principal residence exemption on any of them whenever you sell one. Or you may choose not to claim it and instead claim what's left of your $100,000 capital gains exemption. Or you may combine the two exemptions when you sell one of your properties.

Just remember that the principal residence exemption completely exempts any gain from tax, while a portion of the gain may still be taxable if you claim your $100,000 capital gains exemption. Even if you combine the two, a portion of a gain will still be taxable. It is not possible to realize a gain completely tax-free by combining the two because the principal residence exemption is applied first. If you reduce your gain to $100,000 by using the principal residence exemption, only a portion of that remaining $100,000 gain will be tax-exempt by virtue of the $100,000 capital gains exemption because of the way the phase-out formula is structured.

Second, don't forget that you and your spouse are each entitled to your own $100,000 capital gains exemptions. If you jointly own any of your homes, you should both be able to claim the portion of the exemption that still applies at the time of sale. This may result in a significant reduction in the gain that is subject to tax. Note that joint or co-ownership is essential. You might want to consider switching to joint or co-ownership now in order to maximize your benefit in the event of any future sale.

Third, you are still subject to the normal tax rules discussed earlier, despite what strategies you are thinking of using in order to avoid the full impact of the phase-out of the $100,000 capital gains exemption. For instance, the attribution rules may apply if ownership of a property is switched from one spouse to the other (see Chapter 10). If your spouse has not contributed financially in any way to the house, the attribution rules will likely apply. Of course, your spouse could purchase all or a part of your interest in the home at fair market value, if you received reasonable consideration for the sale.

You may also be subject to the alternative minimum tax (AMT) rules when you claim your $100,000, which means that you may actually end up paying more tax in the year you undertake your strategy than you had planned. However, you receive credit for any extra tax paid under the AMT system and can carry these credits forward for up to seven years to reduce your regular tax.

If you have accumulated any CNILs (cumulative net investment losses — see Chapter 10), your access to the $100,000 capital gains exemption may be restricted to some extent. The application of any CNILs will take place after you do your phase-out calculations described above and attempt to claim the eligible portion of your $100,000 exemption.

Fourth, remember that the deemed disposition rules will likely come into effect when you attempt to transfer your second property to another person or entity. Of course, this is exactly what you want to have happen if you implement one of the strategies. Most of them centre on triggering a disposition for tax purposes and increasing the cost base, while not actually having any cash change hands on the transaction.

Fifth, always bear in mind that almost all the strategies outlined below for minimizing the effects of the phase-out of the $100,000 capital gains exemption involve a cost of some kind. There will likely be professional fees to pay for assessing the strategy in your particular case and for implementation of the plan. There could be on-going fees if a trust or a corporation enters your life, and there may be less tangible and very personal costs involved if you have to make decisions concerning your family.

Finally, do not lose sight of the fact that, while you may be looking for ways to use as much of your $100,000 exemption as possible, you are also in the process of finalizing plans for your retirement financing. Minimizing the effects of the phase-out of the $100,000 capital gains exemption should be a part of those plans, but not at the expense of your future comfort and security. For example, if you think that your cottage could at some future date come into play in funding your retirement income, there may be no point in looking at strategies that transfer ownership of the property to your children while you get nothing in return. Holding on to the cottage yourself, selling it a few years later and "eating" the tax, and ensuring that you and your spouse have sufficient income on which to live comfortably may be the best and most sensible course you can follow.

RECREATIONAL PROPERTY STRATEGIES

Due to the way the rules for phasing out the $100,000 capital gains exemption are constructed, you may be losing out on more and more of the exemption as every month passes. Ideally, you want to stop the erosion while at the same time you minimize other tax costs, maximize your $100,000 exemption, retain control over your property for as long as you want, ensure that all related costs are minimized, and protect your ultimate financial flexibility.

We will just highlight a few of the more popular strategies here. The Deloitte & Touche book by John Budd entitled *Second Property Strategies: Take Advantage of the $100,000 Tax Exemption While You Can,* offers much more detail, and outlines many other strategies not mentioned here.

First, let's look at one strategy that won't work. If you jointly own your second property with your spouse, you cannot sell your half to your spouse, while your spouse sells his or her half to you and expect to claim a portion of the $100,000 capital gains exemption. You have not really done anything to the ownership of the property except to try to step up its cost and use the exemption. The tax authorities won't accept this gambit. There is also probably little point in transferring ownership of your property to a corporation that you control. Yes, you will get to use a portion of your $100,000, but the problems that ensue later could far outweigh any advantages that you gain now. Definitely seek professional advice if you are thinking of such a transfer.

You should also be aware that if you are in financial difficulty, any transfer of the property you undertake will not offer any protection against creditors should they come knocking on your door. Talk to your lawyer or an insolvency specialist if financial problems are looming on the horizon.

TRANSFER TO YOUR SPOUSE

If you transfer ownership of one of your homes, or your interest in the home, to your spouse and elect for the transfer to take place at fair market value, you will get to use a portion of your $100,000 capital gains exemption. Such transfers are relatively easy to accomplish and the cost can be minimal. However, you are using only one spouse's $100,000 exemption and, if the home is jointly owned, protecting only a portion of one-half of the accrued gain. As well, unless you receive fair market consideration on the sale, the attribution rules will apply on any future sale. Consideration could take the form of your spouse's interest in another home, assuming he or she owns all or a portion of it. The major advantage of this type of transfer is that, between the two of you, ownership and control over the property is still retained.

TRANSFER TO CHILDREN

In Chapter 11 on estate planning, we examined a number of methods of transferring ownership of your capital assets to your children, grandchildren, or even great-grandchildren. As you'll recall, such a transfer must be made at fair market value.

Simply gifting the property to the children is probably not advisable unless you trust your children implicitly, do not need the cash from the real estate, and are not planning on using the property extensively in the future. Selling it to them and taking back a demand note payable may be more palatable. If the note pays interest, you may end up with a stream of income. Since you can demand payment on the note at any time, you can set up conditions for your occupancy of the property. Of course, if you do demand payment, your children may just come up with the cash to pay off the note and curtail your use. Selling a partial interest in the property may solve this last problem.

Many couples will consider using a trust for the transfer of the family recreational property to the children. As explained in Chapter 11, trusts allow you to retain control of the property for as long as you desire, but accomplish the tax objectives you set out to achieve. Trusts come in a variety of shapes and sizes for this particular purpose. You should discuss your exact objectives with your professional advisor before committing yourself to the terms of a particular trust.

The transfer of the family recreational property to your children is not without its pitfalls. Obviously, you should first determine if your children want the property, and if they are prepared to put something into it in future years, whether that be money, effort, repairs, or simply occupying it. You should ensure that they understand the costs of owning a second property — after all, they will probably be involved with raising their children, buying a city home, and saving for their kids' education just when you are thinking about giving them more responsibility for ownership of the cottage or chalet.

These are relatively minor problems compared with the difficulties you will have when trying to figure out which, if any, of your children should get the property. If only one or two are to receive ownership, what do you do with the other children? If all of them get it, what kind of sharing or buy-out arrangements do you want to put into place? It is these kinds of details that often prompt parents to simply hold on to a family cottage or other property and see how things work out over the years. The tax savings now may be tempting, but the problems that could arise by trying to implement a specific tax strategy could undermine the whole process.

Remember that if you transfer the property to your children, you are ultimately giving up control of its income-earning potential. If your children own it, you won't be able to put a reverse mortgage on it should you run short of cash a few years after you have retired, and you certainly won't be able to sell it to finance a move across the country or to some sunny southern island.

TRANSFER TO YOUR PARENTS

If your parents are still alive, transferring ownership of one of your properties to them may solve a number of problems. When arranging the transfer, you would rely on their assurances that the property comes back to you via their wills. You may try to institute other safeguards to ensure that you regain ownership when your parents die. You also will want to ensure that you retain control and access to the property during their lifetimes.

One of the most significant advantages of this type of arrangement is that if your parents no longer own their own home, they will be able to use their principal residence exemption to shelter any future gains from tax. Assuming that they do not acquire another home during the rest of their lives, you should eventually inherit the home with no tax payable by your parent's estate.

TIME TO SELL

Of course, you just might want to consider selling one of properties at this time. This isn't a bad time to think about "moving up" to something bigger and better located. The market is still weak in most areas of the country and prices are depressed. This means that you won't get as much for your property, but you'll also pay a lot less for a new one.

RENTAL PROPERTY STRATEGIES

The phase-out of the $100,000 capital gains exemption also applies to rental properties and even vacant land, unless you are using the property in an active business. For your operation to be considered an active business and not an investment, you will generally have to have several properties or a large apartment complex, and employ at least six full-time employees, one of whom may be yourself. If, in the 24 months prior to sale, the property was used in any type of active business carried on by you or a family member, or by a corporation controlled by you or a family member, it may escape the phase-out rules. Typically, you would be leasing such a real property to the business or corporation.

In most cases, a capital gain will result when you sell a rental property for a profit, although in certain circumstances you may be considered to have realized an income gain by the tax authorities and the gain will be fully taxable. You should clarify your position with your tax advisor before negotiating a sale, since your tax situation may influence your asking and final sale price. Capital losses as well as capital gains can be realized when you sell a rental property (losses are not allowed when you sell a personal property such as the family home or recreational property). If you have been claiming CCA (capital cost allowance or tax depreciation), you may also have a recapture of depreciation for tax purposes, which is included in income and taxed at full rates. Special regulations, called the terminal loss rules, apply if you sell the building for a loss, that is, at less than its undepreciated value.

There is actually more scope for triggering a capital gain for tax purposes while retaining control of your rental property than there is for personal real estate. Most of the techniques outlined above for personal residential properties apply to rental properties, including the various transfers to your children. In fact, if your children are attending post-secondary school, or are about to, a transfer of a rental property to them may provide a significant amount of their cash requirements and ease your tax burden.

For example, if you have a rental property that has a relatively low mortgage and is generating large amounts of positive rental income, you might want to transfer part of the ownership to one or more of your children. You must recognize the capital gain on transfer, which is eligible for a portion of your $100,000 capital gains exemption, but after the transfer, your children will be earning a portion of the positive rental income and it will be taxed in their hands, if they are at least 18. That is, there will be no attribution of this rental income to you. If the property is not providing enough income for the children's schooling, they might consider re-mortgaging the property for a higher amount and using the proceeds to augment the financing for the rest of their schooling. They should be aware, however, that the interest payable on this type of loan is not deductible for tax purposes.

If you want to retain control of the property, you should definitely consider using a trust. However, your children may benefit from controlling the property and operating the small rental business. They might even consider living in the home if it is relatively convenient to their school. If you want to retain access to the value of the property, definitely consider taking back a demand note for the fair market value of the rental property at the time you make the transfer to your children, less any debt owing on it and assumed by them. When they have finished school, the property could be sold, any outside debt on it paid off, and most of the remaining proceeds could go to you as payment in full for the note. If they have re-mortgaged the property, you may have to forgive a portion of the note, but this likely will not result in a tax problem. Nor should it turn into a cash-flow problem, since you were going to finance their post-secondary education in any case.

SALE TO A CONTROLLED CORPORATION

Transferring a second property that is used personally by you and your family to a corporation could lead to a number of problems. Transferring an investment property to a corporation that you or family members control may be an ideal solution to using your $100,000 capital gains exemption. Such a transfer might also be done in conjunction with any estate planning that you are undertaking.

The transfer of the rental property to a corporation can be conducted at any amount between cost and fair market value. You would opt to transfer it at or near fair market value to trigger a capital gain. You can establish a new corporation or use an existing one if you already run an incorporated business or have set up a corporation to hold your investment portfolio. Before making the transfer, you want to give careful consideration to the share structure of the corporation. You should ask yourself:

- Do you want to retain control of the property or give control to your children?
- Do you, as a shareholder of the corporation, want to continue receiving the income generated from the property, or do you want it to go to your children?
- Do you want to retain the current value in the rental property and be able to have access to that value at some time in the future?
- Do you want to participate in future increases in value of the rental property, or will your children begin to accumulate these gains as shareholders of the corporation?
- What are the income tax implications of embarking on such a strategy?

To accomplish any of these goals, you would arrange the share structure of the corporation appropriately before making the transfer. In a typical situation, your adult children would subscribe for the common shares of the new corporation and you would then take back voting preferred shares as consideration for the sale of the rental property to the corporation. You would control the corporation through the voting preferred shares, but your children would participate in the future growth in value of the rental property. You could either pay yourself dividends on the preferred shares in respect of the rental income earned by the corporation or forgo the income. At any time, you could set up a redemption program for your shares to augment your retirement income, which would reflect the fair market value of the rental property when it was transferred to the corporation.

Using a corporation gives you a great deal of flexibility, but this comes at a cost. First, if you don't already have a corporation established, you will have to set one up. There will be legal and accounting fees, plus the ongoing expense of tax returns having to be filed every year for the corporation and various other regulations having to be met, many of which involve either a small cost or time on your part. Many taxpayers simply don't want to complicate their lives further by adding a corporation to an already crowded financial plate.

Still, the corporation can be used to accomplish a great variety of goals that you set. Once established, it can be used for much of your estate planning. You can also use it to hold your other investments and reap the benefits of deferral. And it may prove handy for splitting income with your spouse, although this requires considerable planning.

There are a couple of disadvantages to using a corporation. First, if you are not in the top tax bracket, there may actually be some expense involved in flowing corporate income (rental income from the rental property) through to shareholders. This could be a serious problem if your children are in university and you expect to use the rental income to finance their school expenses. Paying them dividends on their common shares probably means that you are paying too much tax. Paying them a salary solves this problem, but the children must perform duties as employees of the corporation in order to justify a salary, and the salary must be reasonable in the circumstances.

It may be difficult and expensive to add children to the shareholder roster if the property appreciates significantly in value. Thus, you generally have to do it right the first time. It is also impossible to transfer the property out of the corporation, other than for fair market value. In other words, while you can transfer property into a corporation at cost, it cannot be transferred back to you at cost. Moving into the property while it is still owned by the corporation is not recommended, since a large taxable benefit will be conferred on one or more of the shareholders, which would not occur if the property were owned personally. And the $100,000 capital gains exemption is not available on property owned by a corporation. However, if the children sell their shares in the corporation, the $100,000 exemption may be available.

Finally, you should investigate whether capital taxes are levied in your province on rental properties owned by a corporation. In some provinces, these levies have been increasing substantially and may push the cost of transferring the property to a corporation over the top.

MOVING INTO YOUR RENTAL PROPERTY

A number of people approaching retirement have acquired properties with the intention of eventually moving into them upon retiring. In the meantime, they have rented the properties and gradually fixed them up to their specifications. Accelerating your decision to move into the property may allow you to use the $100,000 capital gains exemption before the phase-out begins to affect the size of your exempt gain. If you decide to move into a rental property for which you have previously made a claim for CCA, you will be deemed to have disposed of it for tax purposes and must recognize any resulting capital gain. This gain is eligible for a portion of your $100,000 exemption, subject to the phase-out provisions.

Note that if you have not claimed any CCA on that particular property, you have the option of electing for the deemed disposition not to apply. When you eventually sell the property, a portion of the gain will be eligible for your principal residence exemption. You are not allowed to elect for only a portion of the gain to be recognized when you move into the home. It's an all or nothing choice. If you do make the election, you, of course, will continue to suffer from the erosion of your $100,000 capital gains exemption on the gain that accrued to the time you moved into the home.

You might also consider selling your rental property to a third party. In many areas of the country, house prices are not expected to increase very much over the next few years. However, your ability to claim the $100,000 capital gains exemption on any accrued gain will continue to decline. In an extreme case, you may actually be losing money the longer you hold on to the property. This would be the case if you acquired the property in the late 1980s or early 1990s, but before March 1992. You might want to calculate exactly where you stand today and where you might stand in the future. A real estate agent should be able to tell you what kinds of increases in the value of rental properties are expected in the next year or two. However, bear in mind the underlying long-term value of your investment and don't forget to take into account the amount of rental income that you are earning on the property.

Chapter 15 — Foreign Real Estate Planning

More and more Canadians getting ready for retirement are buying homes in southern climes, primarily in the United States. Prices are inexpensive compared with those in many areas in Canada, travel to the southern location is easy, and most discover the winter months to be thoroughly enjoyable. While the lifestyle may sound idyllic, the tax consequences of owning a home in a foreign jurisdiction may not be. If you remain a Canadian resident, you now have two tax systems to deal with, which usually means twice the headaches. Any strategies you may contemplate for relieving potential distress are often complex and costly, and sometimes difficult to implement.

As we noted in Chapter 10, Canadian residents are taxed on their worldwide income. This includes any gains that arise on the sale of foreign real estate. As well, foreign property is subject to the same rules on death as is Canadian property. Thus, when you die and your foreign home goes to someone other than your spouse, it will be deemed to be disposed of at fair market value and any gains must be brought into income in your final tax return in the year of death. Credit is given against Canadian income taxes payable for some or all of the foreign income taxes paid on the transaction in the foreign country. So if a foreign profits tax is levied when you sell your home in another country, a credit is available against Canadian tax payable on the capital gain.

A number of foreign taxes may apply on any specific transaction in the foreign jurisdiction. Depending on the country where your home is located, you may run into profits tax, land speculation tax, foreign ownership tax, succession or death duties, gift tax, special inheritance taxes, or land transfer taxes. The foreign tax situation could have changed dramatically since you bought your property, and there may now even be rules against foreign ownership of your home, which imposes its own obvious limits. Many of these taxes and levies will not be creditable against your Canadian income tax liability, most notably estate and gift taxes, because Canada grants a credit only for income or profits taxes paid in the foreign jurisdiction.

Both the Canadian principal residence exemption and the $100,000 capital gains exemption (which, as explained in the previous chapter, is being phased out for gains on certain real estate) are eligible for you to claim when you dispose of your foreign property. However, you must be a Canadian resident to make either claim. In addition, there may be no point in making the claim or you may be better off making a smaller claim because of the foreign tax that is payable.

HOW THE GAIN ON YOUR PROPERTY MIGHT BE TAXED

For example, assume that you sell your U.S. home and must pay $20,000 in U.S. tax on the gain (all amounts are expressed in Canadian dollars). Your Canadian tax payable on the gain is $30,000 before application of any foreign tax credits. Note that this explanation is greatly simplified and does not necessarily reflect actual tax rates. You will receive credit for the $20,000 of U.S. tax paid, but still owe $10,000 of Canadian tax. Also note that the foreign tax credit mechanism does not necessarily mean that all foreign taxes paid will be creditable against Canadian taxes. You could claim a portion of your principal residence exemption to clear up your Canadian tax bill, but this may not be in your best interests if you also have a Canadian home with large accrued gains. As well, you still have paid $20,000 in foreign tax. That tax cannot be credited toward any other Canadian tax that you may owe in the year.

You also can claim a portion of your $100,000 capital gains exemption, assuming it is still available. However, the tax system is set up so that you first claim a deduction from income for your $100,000 exemption, and then you claim your foreign tax credits against your Canadian income taxes. If you reduce your Canadian tax liability on the gain by one-third ($10,000), generally you also will reduce your access to the foreign tax credit by one-third (down to $13,333), which means that Canadian tax will still be payable.

OTHER TAXES IN THE UNITED STATES

In addition to taxing capital gains, the United States also levies estate and gift taxes. Canadian residents are subject to the U.S. estate tax only on certain assets that are located in the United States at the time of death. Estate tax applies to the value of real estate and certain other assets that are personally owned at the time of death. U.S. residents and U.S. citizens are subject to the same U.S. estate tax on their worldwide assets. Generally, if you are a Canadian resident and not a U.S. citizen, you are not a U.S. resident for U.S. estate tax purposes. Be aware, however, that there are certain exceptions to this general rule. You could be affected if you spend a great deal of time in the United States.

The U.S. estate tax rates range from 18 per cent to 55 per cent. However, the first $60,000 of an estate of a non-resident will generally be exempt from estate tax. The tax is levied on the *fair market value* of the personal property situated in the United States at the time of death, not just on the *gain* that has accrued since it was purchased. Thus, if you purchase an expensive U.S. property and die shortly after the purchase, the estate tax is still payable based on the fair market value of the property. This will occur even if there is no capital gain. If you have a large mortgage, there may not be enough left over from a sale of the property to pay the taxes from the proceeds of sale. If the property is inherited by your children, the tax bill could be substantial enough to force them to sell the property.

As noted in Chapter 11, Canada's "death tax" is really an extension of its capital gains tax. It is not an estate tax. For this reason, any U.S. estate tax payable is not credited against Canadian capital gains tax that may arise on death. Thus, there is the very real possibility of double taxation. The Canadian and U.S. tax authorities are currently trying to establish rules to overcome this problem, but at the time this book went to press, nothing had been finalized.

Note that, upon death, Canadian property can be rolled over to your spouse on a tax-deferred basis and no capital gains will arise until your spouse actually sells the property, or it is inherited by your children from your spouse. In the United States, a limited form of this rollover is available if your surviving spouse is a U.S. citizen and inherits your U.S. property.

As you should have gathered from reading these first couple of pages, just about anybody's situation can vary from straightforward to extremely complex. If your U.S. real property is worth less than $60,000, you do not have that much of a problem, unless you sell it and a gain is realized. By claiming the principal residence exemption or the $100,000 capital gains exemption, you can eliminate most of the Canadian tax. You have little choice over how much U.S. tax you pay. However, if you have substantial assets in a foreign country, you should definitely consider consulting with a professional familiar with both the Canadian tax system and that of the foreign jurisdiction. Fortunately, many tax professionals in Canada are familiar with U.S. taxes and many planning strategies have been developed to overcome potentially serious cross-border tax problems.

SELLING YOUR U.S. PROPERTY BEFORE DEATH

Generally, less tax is payable if you sell your U.S. home while you are still alive than if you die and become subject to the U.S. estate tax. The exact difference depends on the accumulated gain on the home and the current value of the property. Remember, for individuals who are not U.S. citizens, there is a $60,000 exemption on estates. If you are a U.S. citizen or a resident of the United States, the exemption is $600,000.

If you do not sell your property, but rather give it to a family member, the gift will attract U.S. gift tax and also Canadian capital gains tax. However, the U.S. gift tax will not be creditable against the Canadian income tax that must be paid.

The sale of a U.S. property to a family member is deemed to take place at fair market value for both Canadian and U.S. tax purposes. However, in the United States, a withholding tax of 10 per cent of the greater of the fair market value or the purchase price must be remitted to the U.S. Internal Revenue Service (IRS) at the time of sale. This amount is then applied against any U.S. income tax that is owing in respect of any capital gain that arises on the disposition. Such a disposition will have to be reported by filing a U.S. tax return for that year.

The Canada–United States tax treaty may provide relief where a Canadian resident disposes of U.S. property that was acquired before September 1980. Professional advice should be sought in these circumstances.

PRACTICAL POINTER   In both countries, you can defer the payment of a portion of the income tax for a number of years (up to four subsequent years in Canada) if you do not receive the entire proceeds at the time the sale is made. It is essential that you co-ordinate the recognition of capital gains in both countries so as to maximize your U.S. foreign tax credits in Canada in future years.

Selling your U.S. property before you die may eliminate any U.S. estate tax problems. The timing of any sale, however, will be based on many factors, one of which will be the impact of income taxes.

OPTION TO PURCHASE STRATEGY

Ideally, you would like to time the sale of your U.S. property to occur shortly before your death. Obviously, timing is a problem and mistiming the sale could have disastrous tax consequences. Therefore, you might want to consider granting the appropriate family member, usually a child or grandchild, an option to purchase your U.S. real estate. The option would generally be structured so that you, your legal representative, or a person named by power of attorney, could choose to sell the property at a particular time. In other words, the person to whom you grant the option could not choose to exercise before you want to sell, and that person must exercise it at the time of your choosing. These terms would be spelled out in the option agreement as would the price to be paid for the property. This price could be determined by a formula or by reference to appraised values.

You should consult with a lawyer in the state or jurisdiction where your property is situated to ensure that the option agreement is properly structured. As well, you might want to get the same lawyer to draft a power of attorney so that another family member, not the one named in the option agreement, could act on your behalf very quickly should you experience sudden ill-health.

The one disadvantage of this strategy is that if you should die suddenly, the power of attorney might not achieve the desired objectives. If this is a concern, you might consider obtaining accidental death insurance, which should be considerably cheaper than standard life insurance despite your age. The insurance proceeds would be used to pay the U.S. estate tax liability.

LIFE INSURANCE STRATEGY

The most straightforward and most assuring way to minimize the effects of the U.S. estate tax is to acquire sufficient life insurance to finance any tax liability that might arise. Unfortunately, this is not the least expensive strategy. Life insurance gets more expensive the older you get, and at some point will become prohibitively expensive or impossible to obtain. As well, you must either keep more insurance as your home increases in value, or arrange for a policy that has an escalation feature built into it.

JOINT OWNERSHIP STRATEGY

Owning your U.S. home with your spouse may cut your estate tax problems in half, or, at the least, defer the tax to the date of death of the surviving spouse. As in Canada, you will have to establish that your spouse contributed proportionately to the purchase of the home in order to benefit.

PRACTICAL POINTER   In order to benefit from this rollover treatment, the United States requires that the surviving spouse be able to demonstrate that he or she contributed proportionately with personal funds to the acquisition of the property. Thus, it would be wise to assemble the necessary documentation while both of you are still alive.

If you now own the home yourself and want to transfer a part ownership to your spouse, you may become subject to U.S. gift tax. However, there may be an annual exemption on gifts of at least $10,000. For higher-valued homes, you may be able to stagger the gift over several years. Again, this plan is not as uncomplicated as it sounds. Professional advice should be obtained.

NON-RECOURSE MORTGAGE STRATEGY

If you have a non-recourse mortgage on your U.S. property, all or a portion of the outstanding amount of the mortgage at the time the estate tax becomes exigible may be deducted from the fair market value of the property in order to arrive at a value for estate tax purposes. No such deduction is available with respect to a recourse mortgage, even if you have little or no equity in the property. A non-recourse mortgage is one where the lender has access only to the mortgaged property in order to satisfy the debt should the borrower default. The lender cannot go after the personal property of the debtor in the event that the value of the mortgaged property is less than the outstanding amount. As might be expected, lenders are reluctant to issue non-recourse mortgages if they can issue full recourse mortgages. You may end up paying a higher rate of interest on a non-recourse mortgage, especially since you are a non-resident of the United States.

The longer you have the mortgage, the more will be paid off and the less protection the mortgage will offer, since your property is likely going up in value over this period of time. Re-mortgaging periodically for a higher value is a possibility, but it may be expensive. Of course, if you have no need of the mortgage funds, you'll be faced with the prospect of investing them and attempting to obtain a return that at least matches the interest rate on the mortgage. If your return is less than the interest rate, you will be incurring an extra cost for putting this strategy to work for you.

TRANSFER TO A CONTROLLED CORPORATION

Transferring your U.S. home to a Canadian corporation that you control has been a relatively popular way to eliminate the U.S. estate tax. When you die, the corporation continues to own the home and there is no estate tax payable, since you own the shares of the Canadian corporation, not the U.S. real estate. Estate tax is not payable on the shares of the corporation, since it is resident in Canada and you are not a U.S. resident or a U.S. citizen (this technique does not work if you are a U.S. citizen).

Nevertheless, there are a number of disadvantages to this strategy:

• The U.S. tax authorities may "look through" the corporation and ignore it for estate tax purposes, levying the tax on the beneficial owners or the shareholders of the corporation. This is a real possibility if the home earns no rental income and the expenses of owning the home are paid by the shareholders.

- You may be assessed a taxable benefit for Canadian income tax purposes for your personal use of the home now owned by the corporation. This has not been Revenue Canada's administrative policy, as long as the corporation is a "single purpose" corporation, that is, it owns no other assets, all the funds used to acquire the property were supplied by the shareholder, and the property earns no rental income. Unfortunately, these are the conditions that may prompt the U.S. tax authorities to look through the corporation and assess estate tax against the old owners or the shareholders.
- The transfer to the corporation must be undertaken at fair market value for both Canadian and U.S. tax purposes. This means that a capital gain may arise in both countries if the property has been owned for some time. Any U.S. tax paid on the gain should be creditable against Canadian tax owing. Most home owners would prefer to postpone the recognition of any gain and the consequent tax. However, if you have recently purchased the property, there may be little or no gain on it, which alleviates this problem. Note that there is no mechanism for getting the home out of the corporation on a tax-deferred basis at a later date.
- There will be ongoing expenses to maintain the corporation and file Canadian and U.S. tax returns each year.
- As noted earlier, changes might be made to the Canada-United States tax treaty to eliminate the double taxation problem that currently exists. Acting now to transfer your home to a corporation could be an expensive transaction that is difficult to undo without going to further expense.

WHY NOT RENT?

The costs of owning a home in the United States are not inconsiderable. If you make a good investment, these costs may be eliminated with future gains on the property. Still, rents in the sunny south are relatively inexpensive in many areas, especially when compared with the costs of owning a home while not earning any rental income on it.

For many Canadian residents, selling their U.S. vacation property may make a lot of financial sense. If your gain since the date of purchase has been relatively small, the tax liability on a sale should be manageable. Of course, then you are faced with the prospect of renting. However, most renters manage to rent the same place over and over again every year. It won't be as convenient, and you may pay something for summer storage, but you will have eliminated a great deal of the cost of ownership and much of the uncertainty.

If you are planning on living in the south for five or six months of the year every winter, you may prefer owning to renting and may even find the costs comparable. But if you are just spending a month or two in the United States, renting is usually the better deal.

Chapter 16 — Government Benefits and Several Tax Strategies

If you have worked for any length of time in Canada, you should be entitled to Canada or Quebec Pension Plan (C/QPP) benefits, since contributions to the plans are compulsory. If you meet certain residency requirements, you will also be entitled to receive Old Age Security benefits (OAS). These are available to all residents, and in some cases, non-residents, whether or not you have worked for salary or wages in Canada.

WHEN SHOULD YOU RECEIVE YOUR C/QPP?

C/QPP can now be received beginning at any time between the dates you turn age 60 and age 70. However, there is a catch. If you begin to receive your benefits before you turn age 65, they will be reduced by one-half a percentage point for every month you are short of age 65. Thus, if you have just turned age 62 and decide to receive C/QPP benefits, they will be reduced by 18 per cent of the standard benefit that's available the day a person turns age 65. However, if you postpone receiving your C/QPP, your benefits are increased by one-half a percentage point for each month you've gone beyond the date you turn 65. For example, if you have just turned 69, your benefits will be 24 per cent larger than someone who begins to receive benefits the day they turn age 65.

Two other points should be borne in mind. To begin receiving benefits, you must be substantially retired. Generally, you are considered to have retired if your non-retirement income in the year after retiring is less than about 15 per cent of what you were making before you retired. However, you cannot accrue any additional benefits after you turn age 70, whether or not you are retired.

Second, if you begin receiving C/QPP benefits, there is no way to defer tax on the amounts. They cannot be transferred to a pension plan or RRSP. However, note that if you have other qualifying income from a registered pension plan, you are allowed to transfer up to $6,000 of it to a spousal RRSP in each of 1993 and 1994. Thus, by opting to take your C/QPP before you need it, you may still be able to shelter some income in your spouse's RRSP, but only for those two years.

The question is whether you will gain any advantage by taking your C/QPP benefits early rather than waiting until age 65 or later, assuming that you retire early. Generally, receiving those extra payments will prove beneficial, assuming that you do not live longer than normal. In other words if you are male, you will have to live well into your 70s before taking your C/QPP at age 62 and receiving an extra 36 months of payments would not be worthwhile. This is the result, even though those payments are smaller to begin with and will continue to be smaller throughout your retirement than if you had begun receiving them at age 65 or later.

However, with today's low interest rates and our increasing propensity to live longer and longer, you could certainly make a case for delaying receipt of the C/QPP, assuming that you don't need the funds. Of course, any calculations made are based on the assumption that you don't really need the funds and you instead invest them on a compound basis. Whether you are better off delaying or accelerating receipt of C/QPP benefits depends on the assumptions you make about future rates of interest — and of course it also depends on need. If you absolutely need your C/QPP to get your retirement income up to scratch, you are certainly not taking any great risk by arranging early C/QPP. The differences are relatively marginal until one turns about age 80 and depend to a great extent on what you could earn with the funds if that option is open to you.

Note that delaying the receipt of your C/QPP benefits to later than age 65 does not, at least statistically, work to anyone's benefit. You would have to live well into your eighties to begin to see any benefit.

PRACTICAL POINTERS

• If you have been thinking about arranging to receive a retirement income from your RRSP while delaying receipt of your C/QPP, you may be better off reversing your plans. Generally, you would be better off retaining the tax shelter of the RRSP and taking the early C/QPP, assuming that you are able to use your $1,000 pension income tax credit (see later in this chapter).

• If you will be taxed at the low rate of about 27 per cent now, but expect to be pushed into the middle bracket (about 40 per cent) when you begin receiving OAS, you might consider taking your C/QPP early so at least a portion of the benefits are taxed at the lower rate.

As we stressed elsewhere in the book, looking after yourself is at the core of retirement planning. That means enjoying your retirement years as much as you can, while you still can. Taking your C/QPP a few years early will suit many retirees because it frees up a fair amount of cash in the few years immediately after retiring. These are the years of your retirement when you'll be most active and most likely to take advantage of having the extra money.

TIMING THE RECEIPT OF C/QPP BENEFITS

If you will begin receiving your C/QPP toward the end of the year, either beginning receipt just before the end of the year or waiting until January can make a difference in the size of your benefits each year of your retirement. C/QPP benefits are indexed according to increases in the Consumer Price Index (CPI) once a year in January. As well, your starting C/QPP benefit is established based on increases in the yearly maximum pensionable earnings (YMPE), which in turn is based on increases in the average industrial wage. You are affected by this adjustment only once — when you begin to receive benefits.

What this means is that if you begin receiving your C/QPP benefits in December, you are subject to that year's YMPE base, and your January payment will then be indexed according to the increases in the CPI. If you begin receipt of your payments in January, your payment will be based on next year's YMPE, but it won't be adjusted for inflation or increases in the CPI for another year. Thus, the two January payments won't necessarily be the same. If wages have been increasing faster than inflation, you'll be better off waiting until January to receive your first payment. If inflation has been outstripping wage increases, take your first payment in December or earlier. Remember that all future payments you receive will be indexed based on the initial amount you receive. By choosing the higher amount, the extra in your monthly cheques will begin to add up in a few years.

PRACTICAL POINTER   It's generally possible to determine in advance how wage and CPI increases compare and what effect they will have on the January C/QPP benefit. Usually you should be able to get sufficient information with a phone call to the Department of Health and Welfare, which administers the C/QPP, to determine which option is better for you.

Don't forget that by taking your first payment in December instead of January, that payment will be adjusted downward by 0.5 per cent. Take this into account when making your calculations.

SPLITTING YOUR C/QPP BENEFITS BETWEEN YOU AND YOUR SPOUSE

If you expect your tax rate to be higher or lower than your spouse's, the two of you will generally benefit by splitting your C/QPP benefits, assuming that you are not each receiving about the same amount.

If you apply to have your benefits split, a portion will continue to be paid to you and the other portion to your spouse. The amount paid to your spouse is based on the years of marriage. Your spouse will be taxed on the half received by him or her, since there is no attribution of C/QPP benefits. However, both spouses must make the request to split their benefits, each must be at least age 60, and each must have ceased to make contributions to the C/QPP.

At the moment, you must be legally married to apply for split C/QPP benefits. However, according to a proposal in the federal 1992 budget, persons of the opposite sex living common law will be treated as being married in a number of situations for tax purposes. No mention was made that common-law spouses may be treated as married for purposes of splitting C/QPP benefits, although it may find its way into the law books soon.

Note that this program is not available if you have contributed solely to the QPP. However, if you contributed to both the QPP and the CPP, you are eligible to split benefits. If both you and your spouse are entitled to benefits, you both must be at least age 60 before you can begin receiving split benefits. If one did not contribute to the C/QPP, he or she can be under age 60. If your spouse dies, your original benefits will be reinstated. They will not be if your marriage happens to fall apart while you are retired.

COLLECTING YOUR OLD AGE SECURITY

Generally, you must have resided in Canada for at least ten years before you can begin receiving partial OAS benefits. Residency of 40 years entitles you to maximum benefits. Canada has a number of agreements with other countries concerning old age benefits. In some cases, residency in another qualifying country may count toward receiving larger OAS benefits. You may also continue to be entitled to receive OAS even though you are no longer a Canadian resident. In both cases, contact the Department of Health and Welfare to determine if you are eligible and which forms need filling out.

You must apply to receive OAS — it is not automatically paid to you. You cannot begin receiving benefits until you turn age 65. However, the payments do not increase if you delay receipt, so be sure to apply a few months early. The monthly payments are indexed each quarter according to increases in the CPI.

ESCAPING THE OAS CLAWBACK

Higher-income pensioners will discover that what the government sends as an OAS cheque each month goes back to the government as a special tax in April of the following year. This clawback tax is aimed at pensioners whose income exceeds a certain threshold. In 1993, this threshold is $53,215. For every $100 your income exceeds this threshold amount, you must pay back $15 of your OAS benefits as a special tax. The maximum payable is the amount of OAS benefits received in the year. If your net income for tax purposes is below the threshold, the clawback does not apply.

Note that the clawback applies on an individual-by-individual basis. Thus, if your income is $53,215 and your spouse's income is $53,215, there is no clawback of OAS benefits, even though your family income totals $106,430. However, if your income is $80,000 and your spouse's income is $20,000, you will lose all your OAS to the clawback, even though your family income totals only $100,000.

To minimize the effects of the clawback, you have to reduce your income, and the time to start is now. Income splitting always makes sense. If it will get rid of the clawback beast, it makes even more sense. Having the lower-income spouse earn income that the higher-income spouse otherwise would have earned should put you in a better position to avoid the clawback. Review the income splitting section in Chapter 10 and don't forget to take advantage of spousal RRSP contributions. As well, you may be able to lower your income by opting to split C/QPP benefits with your spouse. Bear in mind that you can transfer up to $6,000 of certain pension income you receive to your spouse's RRSP in each of 1993 and 1994.

Most retirees have at least a little flexibility over their income levels. In the year immediately following retirement, you may have a fair amount of RRSP room available for contributing. You'll at least have the ability to contribute in respect of your prior year's income. These deductions may be enough to declaw the clawback for at least a year or two. As well, if you don't need the funds, there is no point in arranging to receive a retirement income from your RRSP and then watch your OAS being clawed back. Postpone your RRSP decision until you turn age 71.

PRACTICAL POINTERS

- If it looks like you will be subject to the clawback, you might consider not contributing to your RRSP in the year or two before retiring, and saving the contribution room for the first two or three years of retirement. You would invest the contributions that you otherwise would have made, so the cash will be available for the contributions later on. This may not make sense if you are currently in the top tax bracket, and the contribution will be deducted later when you are in the middle tax bracket. However, if you will be in the top tax bracket both before and after retiring, it's worth considering.

- If you have made past service contributions to your registered pension plan and are now able to deduct up to $3,500 a year from income in respect of these contributions, you might consider saving the deduction for the period after you retire if you expect to be mauled by the clawback.

- If you have a reasonable degree of control over your income, you might consider arranging for your income to be exceptionally high one year and then lower the next year, to get it below the OAS clawback threshold. You will have to bite the clawback bullet every alternate year, but this is better than being bitten every year.

- You should consider delaying receipt of your C/QPP benefits if you can lower your income and reduce the impact of the clawback. Of course, once you reach age 71, you have no choice but to begin receiving the benefits.

- Many pension plans provide that benefits are reduced once you start receiving OAS benefits. If your OAS is to be clawed back, you could be losing two ways. Talk to your employer now about making adjustments to your pension plan, if possible, if you think that you will be lacerated by the clawback.

THE PENSION INCOME TAX CREDIT

The pension income tax credit can be claimed on your tax return against qualifying pension income, which includes periodic payments from your registered pension plan or DPSP, RRSP, or RRIF retirement income, and annuity income if you are age 65 or older. Note that lump-sum amounts from a pension plan, DPSP, or RRSP do not qualify. Neither do C/QPP or OAS benefits. Individuals who have not reached age 65, but are receiving pension income, can also claim the pension income tax credit.

The credit can be claimed against your taxes owing and will eliminate taxes on a maximum of $1,000 of pension income. The credit is worth about $270 in reduced federal and provincial taxes. If you do not belong to a registered pension plan, be sure that both you and your spouse contribute to RRSPs in order to generate enough income to maximize the credit. Consider using a spousal RRSP if your spouse does not have any earned income for RRSP purposes. Once retired, remember that your spouse can transfer any unused pension credit to your tax return.

PRACTICAL POINTER   If you are age 65 and about to retire, but have no income qualifying for the pension income tax credit, consider "manufacturing" some by acquiring an annuity that pays at least $1,000 annually. Keep in mind the attribution rules if your spouse is also acquiring an annuity. If you buy it for your spouse, or give him or her the money to acquire it, the income from the annuity will be attributed to you.

THE $6,000 RRSP TRANSFER

As we have noted several times, you are eligible to transfer up to $6,000 to your spouse's RRSP in each of 1993 and 1994. The transfer does not affect your normal RRSP contribution limits. However, the transfer may be made only in respect of periodic pension or DPSP income. C/QPP or OAS benefits and RRSP retirement income do not qualify for the transfer. The transfer can be made only to your spouse's RRSP and not to his or her RRIF. Thus, the transfer must be made before the end of the year in which your spouse turns age 71.

You should definitely consider making the transfer if your spouse is taxed at a lower rate than you are. The money that goes into your spouse's RRSP will eventually be paid to your spouse and be taxed in his or her hands at the lower rate, rather than being taxed in your hands at the higher rate.

CHARITABLE GIVING

Many Canadians plan to donate some of their accumulated property to charity at some point. The question is when. Postponing the donation until you die lets you continue to enjoy the property and reduces your taxes on death, but it provides no financial benefit while you are still alive. Donating the property outright now may provide you with large tax credits, but you lose control and use of the property.

There are, however, a variety of strategies available for donating now, getting the financial benefits of the donation, but still retaining some control over the property, which allows you to continue to use and enjoy it, although perhaps not on the same scale that would be available if you had not donated it.

One of the most common methods of donating is to make a charity the beneficiary of a life insurance policy. It may be a fully paid up policy, or one on which you are still paying the premiums. If the policy is fully paid up, your charitable donation for tax purposes will generally be limited to a specific interest in the policy, not the actual face value. This interest is the amount on which your charitable donation tax credit will be based. Generally, if you are still paying the premiums on the policy, you may, depending on your age, be better off transferring ownership of the policy to the charity and then donating the cash value of the premiums each year. These payments will be eligible for the charitable gift tax credit which, like the pension income tax credit, is deducted from your federal tax owing. Since provincial taxes are computed based on federal taxes, except in Quebec, the credit indirectly reduces your provincial income taxes as well. The calculation of the credit is described below.

If you own works of art that could be donated to a gallery or perhaps a piece of real estate that a charitable organization could use in its activities, you might be able to donate a residual interest in the asset to the gallery or charity. You would retain exclusive use of the asset until your death and then it would go to the charity. The agreement would give the charity an irrevocable right to the asset on your death.

The amount eligible for your charitable donation tax credit is the residual interest in the property, that is, the portion of the current value of the property that the charity will eventually receive. The entire current fair market value of the asset is not available for your tax credit since you will continue to enjoy the asset during your lifetime. The residual interest, and therefore the size of your tax credit, depends primarily on your life expectancy.

You also might be able to donate a part interest in an asset, such as a painting or recreational property, to a charity. For example, you could donate a painting to a gallery and share it with the gallery during the year. If you hang it in your home for six months and the gallery gets it for the other six months, you may be entitled to a charitable deduction for half its current fair market value at the time you make the arrangement. Assuming you find a gallery to agree with this type of plan, you also might make the agreement renewable periodically, so that you get to take advantage of the increase in the value of the work of art over time.

These donating techniques can become complex and have a number of pitfalls. You are cautioned to consult carefully with your professional advisor before entering into any type of arrangement.

Generally, you are allowed a combined federal and provincial tax credit of about 27 per cent on the first $250 of a charitable gift in any one year, and about 46 per cent on any amount above $250. The exact percentages depend on the province in which you live and its tax rates. The donation on which your tax credit is based in any one year for gifts to most charities is limited to 20 per cent of net income for tax purposes. Unused donations can be carried forward five years.

Donations to the Crown are not subject to the 20 per cent limitation. Generally, when donating capital property, you can choose a value for the donation anywhere between your cost and the asset's current fair market value. As a result, a gain may arise upon donating a valuable work of art, for instance, to a gallery, and you choose a value that is close or equal to the fair market value of the asset. This gain may be offset by your $100,000 capital gains exemption and, as well, you receive a large credit against your taxes owing from making the gift. If you donate qualifying Canadian cultural property, you are deemed to have donated it at its current fair market value, but you do not have to report the capital gain for tax purposes.

TAXES ON FOREIGN PENSIONS

The Canadian tax rules on foreign pension benefits paid to you and those of the foreign jurisdiction can be complex. If Canada has a tax treaty with the country from where the pension is paid, preferential treatment usually applies to the pension payments. Government payments may be partly exempted from tax, and a low rate of withholding tax, or none at all, may apply when the payments are made from the other country to you. Pensions from countries with which Canada does not have a tax treaty are usually treated less generously.

PRACTICAL POINTER   Before you retire and begin collecting foreign pension income of any type, you should consult with your professional advisor to determine the tax status of the income. Bear in mind that, as a Canadian resident, you are taxed on your worldwide income and receive credits against your Canadian tax liability for some or all of the foreign taxes paid on the benefits.

Generally, Canada applies the same rules to foreign pension income that it applies to domestic pension income. If the contributions to the foreign plan were deductible and the income was tax-sheltered, the entire amount of the pension will be taxable in Canada when received. However, if contributions were not deductible, or if the income was not fully tax-sheltered, a portion or all of the income may escape Canadian tax. Different rules generally apply to government pension income.

Your foreign pension income must be converted to Canadian dollars, either at the rate in effect at the time the income was received or at the average rate during the year. This average is available from Revenue Canada shortly after the end of the year.

U.S. SOCIAL SECURITY AND OTHER U.S. PENSIONS

Presently, U.S. Social Security benefits paid to a Canadian resident are not subject to tax in the United States and only one-half the amount received is taxed in Canada.

Pension income derived from U.S. IRA and Keogh accounts (retirement vehicles similar to RRSPs) and company pension plan payments are subject to special withholding rates in the United States. Such amounts are fully taxed in Canada, but are generally eligible for the $1,000 pension income tax credit.

Chapter 17 — Retiring Outside of Canada

Retiring outside of Canada certainly has its attractions. The climate almost certainly will improve, at least during the winter. You may have more opportunity to travel and become familiar with new places and cultures, and you may be financially better off retiring in a country with a more hospitable tax climate.

On worldwide standards, Canadians are taxed relatively heavily. However, we receive a considerable amount for our taxes, including comprehensive and, in most cases, excellent health care, a wide variety of benefits specifically designed for seniors, and a government-sponsored security net that ensures that virtually no one slips between the cracks. Canada is considered to be one the best places to live in the world when one factors in the services, conveniences, and luxuries we take for granted. Our standard of living is high and enjoyable, although we certainly do pay for it.

Still, many Canadians reflecting on their retirement years also think of southern climes, low tax rates, and 12 months of golf. Many Canadian residents are citizens of another country, and many are from the United States and plan to return once they retire. This chapter deals with those, including U.S. citizens, who intend to pull up roots and settle in the United States or another country. In Chapter 14, we dealt with those who want to spend a few months down south, but who are likely to run into real estate and estate tax problems. This chapter looks at the planning that is essential if you are considering taking up permanent residence outside Canada.

The process of uprooting yourself from Canada can be just as challenging as settling in a new, unfamiliar land. You likely have assets in Canada on which tax has been deferred, such as your

RRSPs or pension plans, real estate, and a variety of investments. Canada wants to collect that tax in one way or another, and, of course, you want to minimize any current and future tax liability. You probably also want to retain some ties with Canada. Perhaps you want to spend summers here with your children, or ski for a month or two at Whistler. Canada taxes its residents on their worldwide income, but, once you leave, the last thing you want is to still be considered a Canadian resident for tax purposes. Escaping Canada's high tax rates is probably close to the top of the list of reasons why you are contemplating leaving the country.

We assume that you have done your research, know which country you are going to, and have taken care of, or will be taking care of, all the entry requirements. It's no longer easy to pick your favourite country, pack your bags, and retire there for the rest of your life. Most require you to be gainfully employed in the new country, be sponsored by relatives, or be quite wealthy and willing to leave a great deal of your wealth on deposit in the new country. We also assume that you have taken account of what you will be leaving behind. The social security net and health care system come first to mind. But you may also discover that you become restricted in your travel back to Canada and your stays here. You may have to give up control of the family recreational property in order to maintain your non-resident status for purposes of the Canadian tax system. Also, you will likely have a tough time getting back into Canada if you give up Canadian citizenship.

ARE YOU OR AREN'T YOU A RESIDENT OF CANADA?

Revenue Canada has never issued hard and fast rules for determining exactly when a person who leaves Canada becomes a non-resident for tax purposes. As the taxman says, "it's a question of fact". However, guidelines for determining residency have been provided in a number of government tax publications. In very general terms, you must:

- be absent from Canada for at least 24 consecutive months, once you have moved from Canada;
- reside outside Canada for at least six months every year;

- have severed most residential ties with Canada; and
- have become a resident of another country.

Most Canadians who have retired, or are about to retire, and are planning to emigrate from Canada will likely have some problem establishing that they are indeed no longer Canadian residents. Few retirees will sell everything, move to a new country, and have nothing whatever to do with Canada again. Your children and their families are probably still here, as well as other members of your and your spouse's family. You will want to visit, perhaps often. You will want to retain the family cottage or ski chalet and use it periodically during the year, perhaps often. You may want to retain membership in recreational clubs, keep some of your investments, stay involved in some of your volunteer activities, and perhaps even conduct business here on a part-time basis. The extent of your continued involvement with Canada determines your residency for Canadian tax purposes.

Generally, you must sell your year-round permanent Canadian home. If you don't, it must be rented on an arm's-length basis and the rental agreement must provide that you need to give at least three months' notice before you are able to reoccupy the dwelling. If you retain ownership of a "four-season" recreational property, it too generally must be rented on the same basis.

Other residential ties should also be severed or put on a non-resident basis. Personal property, such as automobiles, should be removed from Canada or sold. Bank accounts and Canadian credit cards, as opposed to international cards, should be cancelled. Club memberships should be cancelled or put on a non-resident basis. Everyone with whom you have had financial dealings should be notified that you are becoming, or have become, a non-resident.

Finally, you must be careful of prolonged return visits to Canada. Revenue Canada has stated that spending the summer at a cottage in Canada could jeopardize your non-residency status, although this will not be the only determining factor if push comes to shove. Occasional personal visits to your family will have no effect on your status; nor will relatively short visits to conduct business or look after your investments.

Note that, before you leave Canada, you can request Revenue Canada to provide a determination of your proposed non-residency. However, this determination is not binding on the tax authorities, especially if your circumstances change from those outlined in your request. The request is made on form NR73, Determination of Residency Status, which is available from your district taxation office.

Finally, bear in mind that you could end up being a resident of two countries at the same time. This could result in serious tax consequences, although a tax treaty between the two countries, if one exists, could alleviate most if not all your problems.

LEAVING CANADA — HOW ARE YOU TAXED?

Generally, you cease to be a resident of Canada for tax purposes at the time you leave the country, if, of course, you remain resident in another country for at least two years. This does not mean that you are no longer subject to Canadian tax. First, you may become subject to tax as a consequence of giving up your Canadian residency. Second, you will continue to be subject to Canadian tax on most income received from Canadian sources, and on almost all income earned in Canada.

At the time you leave Canada, you may become subject to the so-called departure tax. There is no specific tax on individuals leaving Canada. However, if you become a non-resident, you will be deemed to have disposed of all your capital property, with certain exceptions, at fair market value immediately before you become a non-resident. These deemed dispositions will result in any inherent gains or losses being realized. You will then be liable for tax on any net gains that have accrued to that point. The assets that you will be deemed to have disposed of include most marketable securities, such as shares and bonds, real estate situated outside Canada, and most types of personal-use property such as boats, motor homes, automobiles, etc. The tax becomes payable when you file your tax return for your final year of Canadian residence. These gains are eligible for your $100,000 capital gains exemption, and qualifying gains on the sale of shares in private Canadian corporations or qualified farm property may be eligible for the larger $400,000 exemption (see Chapter 12). Any CNILs (see Chapter 10) that you have accumulated may reduce your access to the exemptions.

Assets defined as "taxable Canadian property" are not subject to the deemed disposition rules. Such property includes shares of private Canadian corporations, real estate situated in Canada, accrued pension benefits, and RRSPs and DPSPs. Such property generally cannot be removed from Canada without being sold or disposed of in some manner, which in turn triggers a tax liability that the government has the power to enforce.

Note that special rules apply to persons who have been residents of Canada for less than 60 months in total during the 10-year period preceding departure from Canada. In these circumstances, the deemed disposition rules may not apply to property that the person owned when he or she originally became a Canadian resident.

PRACTICAL POINTER You are permitted to elect for the deemed disposition rules not to apply, and for any or all your assets to be treated as taxable Canadian property. This has the effect of deferring Canadian tax until the assets are actually sold. You generally must post acceptable security with Revenue Canada. Usually, a letter of credit will suffice. The election is made on form T2061.

You would not want to make this election for all your property if you have not used up all your capital gains exemption, or if you have losses on hand that can offset some or all of your inherent gains. Remember that you must be a Canadian resident to take advantage of the exemption. It is not available once you leave the country and become a non-resident.

PRACTICAL POINTER You are also allowed to elect for your taxable Canadian property to be deemed disposed of at the time you leave Canada. You would usually want to make this election to take advantage of the $100,000 capital gains exemption and the $400,000 exemption. This also has the effect of increasing your cost of the property, which should result in less tax being paid both in Canada and possibly in your new country of residence when the asset is eventually sold. For example, if you are taking up residence in the United States, there are provisions in the Canada–United States tax treaty which, as explained later, may allow you to increase the cost of the property for U.S. tax purposes.

Note that when making either election, losses resulting from deemed dispositions can only be used to offset gains resulting from deemed dispositions.

Special rules apply when, as a non-resident, you eventually sell taxable Canadian property. Generally, the purchaser must withhold tax equal to one-third of the *purchase price* from the proceeds and remit this to Revenue Canada. On the other hand, you are allowed to notify the government of the impending sale and pay tax equal to one-third of the *capital gain*, or post acceptable security for the potential tax liability. The government will then issue a clearance certificate and the purchaser will not have to withhold any tax. You will always be better off, from a cash flow point of view, to obtain the clearance certificate. Tax on the gain will always be less, possibly much less, than the withholding tax on the purchase price. Nevertheless, you still must file a tax return in the year of the sale and calculate the appropriate amount of tax. Any overpayment will be refunded to you.

When you file your final tax return in the last year of residence, you must report all income earned worldwide from January 1 of the year to the day in the year you leave Canada for good. As well, you must report all income earned in the remainder of the year that is employment or business income or gains on the sale of taxable Canadian property. Your personal tax credits in the year will be prorated depending on the number of days in the year you resided in Canada, but deductions for pension and RRSP contributions will not be prorated.

HOW ARE YOU TAXED IN CANADA WHILE YOU ARE A NON-RESIDENT?

You will generally be required to pay Canadian tax at the regular rates if you:

- earn employment income from duties performed in Canada;
- earn business income from a business carried on in Canada; or
- realize capital gains from the disposition of taxable Canadian property.

You must file a tax return and you will be allowed to claim only a limited number of tax credits and deductions. However, if at least 90 per cent of your worldwide income is from Canadian sources, you will be allowed to claim standard personal tax credits and a larger variety of deductions. Tax will be withheld by employers, and instalment payments on business income must be made in the normal manner. Foreign tax credits are not allowed for any foreign tax that you may owe on this Canadian-source income, but the Canadian tax may be allowed as a foreign tax credit in the other country. If the country in which you are now resident has a tax treaty with Canada, the provisions of the treaty may override the general rules and alter your tax situation. You should consult with your professional advisor to determine your potential status.

PENSION AND RETIREMENT INCOME

If you receive pension and retirement income from sources in Canada while you are a non-resident, tax may be withheld from the amounts. Generally these amounts include:

- pension benefits;
- retiring allowances;
- supplementary pension or unregistered pension benefits;
- DPSP amounts and payments;
- employee death benefits;
- RRSP amounts and RRIF amounts and payments;
- RRSP annuities;
- alimony payments.

Note that some of these amounts may be exempt from withholding tax under tax treaties that Canada has signed with a number of other countries.

PRACTICAL POINTER   **You can elect to file a tax return and report the income items listed above. If the total of these items equals at least 50 per cent of your total worldwide income, you may claim a variety of deductions and personal tax credits on your Canadian tax return. However, because of the complexities involved in calculating your tax liability under new rules introduced in 1990, your credits and deductions could be limited.**

If your Canadian and foreign incomes are split about fifty-fifty, you should determine the exact proportion and see if you are eligible to file a

Canadian return and claim personal exemptions. In some cases, you may eliminate much, and perhaps all, of your Canadian tax that otherwise could be withheld on certain items at the rate of 25 per cent.

No Withholding on Certain Pension Amounts

Most pension benefits and payments or amounts from RRSPs, RRIFs, DPSPs, and retiring allowances are subject to withholding tax. This tax may be allowed as a credit against tax payable in the foreign jurisdiction of which you become a resident. There is no Canadian withholding on the following amounts:

- Old Age Security, or a similar pension paid by a provincial government;
- C/QPP benefits;
- pension benefits that would not be taxable in Canada, such as war veterans' allowances; and
- pension benefits relating to services rendered outside Canada.

As well, a number of tax treaties that Canada has signed with various countries exempt certain pension benefits from withholding tax. Note that your entitlement to OAS depends on your Canadian residency. Your benefits could be eliminated or reduced if you emigrate to another country, although special social security agreements with certain countries may enable you to continue receiving OAS benefits.

Special situations concerning various forms of retirement income and other assets, especially as they relate to emigrating to the United States, are discussed below.

CANADIAN INVESTMENT INCOME

As well, tax is withheld on most types of investment income, stock options, and a variety of other types of income that are neither employment nor business related, or are not gains arising on the disposition of taxable Canadian property. You have no option to file a Canadian return in respect of these income items, and simply must suffer the withholding tax. Your new country of residence may offer foreign tax credits in respect of the Canadian tax, or that country may have a tax treaty with Canada, under which the withholding rate is reduced.

No Withholding on Certain Canadian Investment Income

Income from certain Canadian investments escapes the withholding tax requirement when the investments are owned by non-residents. The list includes:

- government of Canada bonds;
- Canada or Quebec savings bonds purchased before leaving Canada;
- government of Canada treasury bills;
- provincial and municipal bonds;
- certain "long-term" corporate bonds;
- deposits denominated in Canadian currency in the branch of a Canadian bank situated outside Canada; and
- deposits denominated in foreign currencies in any branch of a Canadian bank.

PRACTICAL POINTER   If you wish to continue to hold Canadian investments, you may avoid Canadian withholding tax by owning any of the above securities. They are all relatively conservative, but ownership of any should accomplish at least some of your investment goals. Of course, the income you earn on the investments could quite likely be subject to tax in your new country of residence.

RENTAL INCOME

If you have rental income from Canadian sources after you have become a non-resident, it is subject to withholding tax of 25 per cent on the gross amount. However, as explained later in this chapter, you may be able to calculate the amount of tax to be withheld based on your net rental income, that is, gross income less all applicable expenses.

DEPARTURE STRATEGIES

In the year you leave Canada, there is a variety of planning opportunities that you should definitely consider. Some could be worth literally thousands of dollars in reduced taxes. We stress once again that if your financial affairs are at all complex, you should seek professional tax advice. By leaving Canada, you are dealing with the tax systems of two countries, each of which is likely quite different and will have a different impact on your eventual financial situation. Tax professionals can help you make the two systems work together to your benefit.

Since the greatest number of Canadians leaving the country settle in the United States, we will refer to the United States and possible U.S. tax consequences in many of the strategies outlined below. At the end of the chapter, we include a few words on problems that U.S. citizens now resident in Canada and planning to return to the United States may face.

GIVING UP CANADIAN RESIDENCE AT THE RIGHT TIME

Canadian tax rates are graduated, and it is likely that those of the country to which you will be emigrating are also graduated. By timing the day of your departure properly, you should be able to take advantage of the lower tax rates in each country. In Canada, you will only be taxed on the income you earn in Canada prior to your departure, although after departing you could still be subject to withholding tax on Canadian-source income, and even income tax if you still earn employment or business income in Canada or dispose of taxable Canadian property in the year. Similarly, your new country of residence may only tax you on income earned while you are a resident of that country, not on your total income earned during the year.

PRACTICAL POINTER   If you have AMT (alternative minimum tax) credits outstanding because you were subject to the AMT in a previous year, you should definitely consider trying to use them before you leave Canada. If you cannot use your AMT credits, they could expire unused. Thus, in the year you leave or the year before you leave, you might want to

reduce your reliance on various tax shelters or other investments and claims that reduce your income and make you subject to the AMT. In particular, if you have not used up your $100,000 capital gains exemption, you should ensure that you use it well before leaving Canada, so that your AMT credits can be used in the year or two before you actually leave. Or you should use the exemption when you dispose of taxable Canadian property or other assets when leaving the country. As well, you should arrange for a retiring allowance not to be received and transferred to your RRSP in a year when you are trying to use up previous years' AMT credits.

Note that the AMT applies in the year you give up Canadian residence and file your final tax return. The $100,000 capital gains exemption and deductions for RRSP contributions are not allowed as deductions when calculating AMT, so you could quite likely be subject to the tax in the year you leave Canada since you will be trying to maximize this exemption. It appears that AMT credits can be used to reduce your tax bill if you file a Canadian tax return while you are a non-resident. However, AMT credits can be carried forward for only seven years.

DEALING WITH YOUR CANADIAN PRINCIPAL RESIDENCE

As a general rule of thumb, you are probably better off selling your principal residence (as opposed to a recreational home) in the year you leave Canada or the immediately following year. The reasons why are relatively straightforward. Unfortunately, not everyone wants to follow this course of action, since they think that at some point they may want to return to Canada.

As you are aware from the discussion in Chapter 13, gains on your principal residence are tax-free. The exemption calculation is performed on a year-by-year basis. The important point to note is that to claim the exemption for any particular year, you must be a Canadian resident. Thus, you should at least consider selling your home in the year you leave, or the year after. The "plus 1" in the exemption formula gives you this extra year to arrange the sale, although if you own a second property, such as a cottage or a ski chalet, you may want to save the extra year for any gains that arise on its eventual sale (see below). Remember that if you sell your home after leaving Canada, the purchaser will have to withhold tax on the sale proceeds, unless you obtain a tax clearance certificate from Revenue Canada.

However, note that, if you are planning to settle in the United States, waiting to sell your principal residence, or any real estate for that matter, could eventually cost you sizeable tax dollars. The United States does not allow tax-free gains on the sale of a principal residence, although they do allow the gain to be rolled over or deferred if you acquire another home within a certain time of selling one. You also have a once-in-a-lifetime exemption on gains that you can claim after you turn age 55, but this may not cover the gain on your Canadian home. Thus, once you take up U.S. residence, you could, on selling your Canadian principal residence, be liable for U.S. tax. For a U.S. citizen, the entire gain may be taxable. For an individual who is not a U.S. citizen and who owned his or her home at the time of departure from Canada, only that portion of the gain that accrues after leaving Canada is taxable in the United States. Since there will be little or no Canadian tax payable on the sale, you will not be entitled to any foreign tax credits to offset any U.S. tax that may be payable.

RENTING OUT YOUR PRINCIPAL RESIDENCE

As noted earlier in this chapter, your non-residence status will not be affected if you rent your home after you leave Canada, as long as you cannot cancel your lease without at least three months' notice. If you rent out your property, the *gross* rent charged is subject to withholding tax at the rate of 25 per cent. The tenant is required to remit this to Revenue Canada. However, you can elect to be taxed on your rental income as if you were a Canadian resident. In this case, withholding is limited to 25 per cent of the *net rental* income. Since you will undoubtedly have a variety of expenses associated with renting the property, you will always be better off making the election and opting for the lower withholding.

If you make the election, you must file a Canadian tax return reporting the rental income within six months of the end of the year. No personal tax credits are allowed to be claimed on this return. The difference between tax payable as a result of filing the return and withholding tax already paid to government is reconciled, and will result in you paying the balance of tax owing or receiving a refund because too much tax was withheld. If you don't make the election, you can still file a tax return reporting the rental income. This return must be filed within two years following the year in which the rental income was earned. Filing in this case should result in a refund of much of the 25 per cent tax that was withheld from *gross* rental receipts.

Note that the election, on form NR6, must be filed annually before the beginning of the rental year in question in order to qualify for the 25 per cent withholding on *net rental* income. Also note that if the home is jointly owned, both owners must make the election and file tax retuns.

If you rent your principal residence, you will be deemed to have disposed of it at fair market value at the time the rental commenced. However, no tax liability will result if you are claiming the property under the principal residence exemption rules. If you return to Canada and subsequently move into the home, you will be deemed to have disposed of the property again, and could be liable for any tax on the gain. However, you are permitted to make an election upon leaving Canada that, in effect, allows your home to continue to be treated as a principal residence and therefore not be deemed disposed. If you return to Canada and move back into the home, tax on the portion of the gain not exempted under the principal residence rules will be deferred until the home is actually sold.

If you plan to retain real estate in Canada and you are shifting your residence to the United States, you should thoroughly investigate the income, estate, and gift tax consequences that could arise in the future. Chances are that your Canadian property will form part of your taxable estate, and tax could eventually be payable. However, as a U.S. resident, you would have a $600,000 exemption on the taxable value of your estate, not just $60,000 as a Canadian resident (U.S. estate and gift taxes were discussed briefly in Chapter 14). More importantly, you may be subject to U.S. gift tax, which could seriously impair your ability to transfer ownership of a vacation property or any other type of property to your children.

SHOULD YOU HANG ON TO YOUR RECREATIONAL OR VACATION PROPERTY?

As noted earlier in the chapter, your non-residency status could be jeopardized if you continue to own and use for extended periods each year a vacation property that is situated in Canada. Unfortunately, this is exactly what many Canadians plan on doing after they have emigrated from Canada. The south may be delightful during the winter, but unbearable in the summer. Three or four months at the cottage simply continues a tradition that has been going on for probably five or six decades.

Renting out the cottage on an arm's-length basis and not being able to use the property because of the restrictions in the rental or lease agreement obviously does not solve your dilemma. The best solution may be to transfer ownership of the vacation property to your children *before* you leave Canada. As explained in Chapter 14, you should consider this course of action in any case, if you have not yet used up your $100,000 capital gains exemption and you have substantial accrued gains on the property. A number of strategies for transferring ownership but retaining control over the property were outlined in that chapter. Most will involve a small, or perhaps not so small, immediate tax cost, depending on the size of your gain, how much of your $100,000 capital gains exemption remains, and whether you want to use your principal residence exemption to shelter any of the gain.

CONTRIBUTE TO YOUR RRSP IN THE YEAR YOU LEAVE CANADA

For the year you leave Canada, you must file a tax return reporting, among other items, all the income you earned in Canada while still a resident. You are allowed the full normal deduction for contributions made to your RRSP during this period, within your limits, whereas your personal tax credits will be prorated based on your period of Canadian residency. Thus, it makes sense to maximize your RRSP contributions in the year you leave, especially if you are settling in a country with a more hospitable tax climate, such as the United States.

Generally, you will leave Canada with some RRSP contribution room still available. This can be carried forward up to seven years. It is important to pay attention to this contribution room since you may be able to make use of it if, as a non-resident, you file a Canadian tax return for one of the several reasons which we mentioned earlier in this chapter. Or, if you return to Canada within a few years, you may still be able to make the claim when you file your first tax return as a resident.

If you know that you will be returning to Canada or you will be filing a return while a non-resident in which you can claim RRSP contributions, you might consider making the RRSP contribution in respect of your excess contribution room prior to becoming a non-resident of Canada. As long as the contribution has been made, you can claim the deduction at any time — there is no seven-year carry-forward limit. The contribution will earn tax-sheltered income in the RRSP during this period, at least for Canadian tax purposes. Note that the United States considers this income taxable unless you file an appropriate election (see below).

MAKING THE MOST OF YOUR RRSP RETIREMENT INCOME

Once you leave Canada, withdrawals from your RRSP, as opposed to receiving retirement income, will be subject to Canadian withholding at the rate of 25 per cent. Similarly, retirement income paid in the form of an annuity or amounts paid out of your RRIF will also be subject to withholding. However, the standard rate of 25 per cent may be reduced by a tax treaty between Canada and your new country of residence. For example, if you settle in the United States, the withholding rate is 15 per cent. This is much lower than the rate you would pay if you were still a Canadian resident.

PRACTICAL POINTER   If you are emigrating to the United States and certain other lower-tax-cost countries, there is no point collapsing your RRSPs before you leave Canada. Generally, you will be able to receive retirement income less expensively if you leave your RRSPs intact. This is a departure from advice that was given a number of years ago when tax law

here and in other countries, most notably the United States, favoured the collapsing of RRSPs before departure.

Of course, your RRSP retirement annuity income or payments from your RRIF will be subject to tax in your new country of residence. However, in the United States, the tax regime is extremely favourable. The United States recognizes only the income earned in the RRSP since taking up U.S. residence as being taxable. Thus, if you move to the United States and your RRSPs are worth $200,000, this will all be considered non-taxable capital for U.S. tax purposes. Only the income earned in the RRSP and any capital gains realized in your plans will be subject to tax on a current basis. Two important points should be noted:

- Since the United States will at some point tax capital gains realized in your RRSP after taking up U.S. residence, you should consider selling all your winners in your RRSPs before you leave Canada. This could save some individuals a considerable amount of U.S. tax, although in the long run it may not make much difference to most because RRSPs are so lightly taxed in the United States.
- Since 1985, you have been allowed to elect for U.S. tax purposes that income earned on contributions made to your RRSP while you were a Canadian resident not be subject to U.S. tax until it is distributed. In other words, if you make the election, no tax will be exigible on the income earned in your Canadian RRSPs until it is actually received as annuity income or as payments from an RRIF, and then, only the income earned or gains realized since becoming a U.S. resident will be subject to tax.

It is extremely important that you make this election. Besides deferring U.S. tax, it also sets up the possibility that you will be able to fully use your foreign tax credits for Canadian withholding tax to offset any U.S. tax that is eventually payable. For example, when you eventually begin to receive RRSP annuity income or RRIF payments, Canadian tax will be withheld at the rate of 15 per cent. U.S. tax will also be payable, but only on a small fraction of the actual amounts being received. Chances are good that credits you receive in respect of the Canadian withholding tax will easily offset any U.S. tax for which you are liable. In other words, you may end up paying tax at the rate of only 15 per cent on your RRSP instead of at rates as high as 50 per cent if you had remained in Canada.

DECISIONS ABOUT YOUR PENSION INCOME

Income received from registered pension plans while you are a non-resident is treated much the same as RRSP income. Lump-sum payments are subject to withholding at 25 per cent, but Canadian tax on periodic payments could be withheld at the lower 15 per cent rate, depending on whether Canada has a tax treaty with the country in which you plan to take up residence. This is the case with the United States.

However, the United States treats Canadian-source pension income a little differently from RRSP retirement income. It treats your and your employer's contributions to the plan as capital and therefore not taxable, but all income and gains earned in the plan are taxable for U.S. purposes when received by you. Such income and gains are not taxable if you have not begun to collect your pension, so there is no need to make an election as there is with your RRSPs.

PRACTICAL POINTER Since U.S. tax on your registered pension plan income could be considerably higher than on your RRSP annuity income and RRIF payments, you might consider transferring your accumulated pension plan benefits to your RRSP before you leave Canada and emigrate to the United States. These pension amounts will lose their identity for U.S. tax purposes, and be regarded as RRSP amounts, none of which are taxable for U.S. purposes immediately after you take up U.S. residence. Only the income earned on those amounts will eventually become subject to tax.

This strategy will also appeal to those who have no real need of their pension income immediately upon taking up residence in the United States. They will be able to continue to shelter income inside the RRSP for both Canadian and U.S. tax purposes, and won't have to arrange to begin receiving retirement income until the year they turn age 71. Of course, you should ensure that the retirement income that you eventually receive from your RRSP is equivalent, more or less, to the benefits that you would expect to receive from your pension plan. This could prove to be quite a complex calculation.

PRACTICAL POINTER In the year or two before you leave Canada, you should make every attempt to maximize contributions and benefits available under registered pension plans. As noted in Chapter 5, you may have opportunities to make past service contributions or buy upgrades to your plan. These amounts are deductible by you and your employer when contributed to the plan, and, when eventually received in the form of pension benefits, could be subject to Canadian tax at rates as low as 15 per cent. If you receive the amounts as salary in the year or two before retiring, you could be paying tax at rates as high as 50 per cent.

INCOME FROM GOVERNMENT SOURCES

As noted earlier in this chapter, there is no Canadian withholding on C/QPP benefits and OAS payments when you receive them as a non-resident. Before leaving Canada, you might want to look into how you will fare with OAS once you leave Canada. The federal Department of Health and Welfare handles such enquiries. If your finances are fairly tight and you are counting on full OAS benefits, you don't want to be surprised and see them cut off after you have severed all ties with Canada. You are entitled to receive your eligible C/QPP benefits no matter where you live or how long you resided in Canada.

One surprise you may discover as a non-resident recipient of OAS is that you will not be subject to the clawback, and, depending on your new country of residence, may not even be subject to any tax on your benefits. The clawback (see Chapter 16) only applies if you file a Canadian tax return.

PRACTICAL POINTER If, as a non-resident of Canada, you are filing a Canadian tax return and in it you must report any OAS received during the year, you should first consider the effects of the clawback if you are reporting a substantial amount of income. The clawback may, in very particular circumstances, make filing the return uneconomic, assuming that you have an option of whether or not to file.

If you are taking up residence in the United States, you will be pleased to learn that only one-half of your Canadian-source government benefits will be subject to tax. They are taxed on the same basis on which U.S. Social Security is taxed, that is, only one-half need be reported for tax purposes. Combined with the lower tax rates in the United States and the fact that there is no Canadian withholding, benefits from the Canadian government will be taxed at substantially lower rates in the United States.

CANADIAN INVESTMENT INCOME

Once you become a non-resident of Canada, tax will be withheld from most types of investment income earned and capital gains realized in Canada. You will also likely be taxed on the income in your new country of residence, although you may be eligible for tax credits for any Canadian tax paid. Earlier in this chapter, we noted several types of income that are not subject to Canadian withholding tax, and we also noted that you can elect for most types of assets to be treated as taxable Canadian property, which may entitle you to better tax treatment when you finally sell the assets and realize gains.

You should note two important points. First, as a non-resident of Canada, you are no longer entitled to the $100,000 capital gains exemption on any gains you realize on the disposition of assets in Canada. Even though you may file a Canadian tax return, the exemption will not be available. Second, if you own Canadian shares and are paid dividends, as a non-resident you will not be able to take advantage of the dividend tax credit mechanism, which acts to reduce the rate of tax on such dividends. You simply must suffer the withholding tax at 25 per cent, or perhaps 15 per cent if a tax treaty is in effect, and hope that you gain credit for the Canadian tax paid when you file a return in your new country of residence. This situation is much the same as if you were a Canadian resident earning dividends on, for example, U.S. shares.

You should review the comments made earlier in the chapter concerning the options you might have for filing a Canadian tax return in any particular year that you are a non-resident. In some circumstances, you may pay less tax, although if your income is substantial, you will generally be better off suffering the Canadian withholding tax.

If you have stock options outstanding upon retirement and are planning on taking up residence in another country, you should thoroughly research your situation with a knowledgeable tax professional. From a Canadian perspective, you will be taxed in the normal manner (see Chapter 6). However, the United States, for one, taxes stock options quite differently. If the options are still outstanding when you take up residence in the United States, you might discover that you have become subject to tax that you were not expecting. In some situations, you may be better off exercising the options before you leave Canada.

Finally, Canada taxes capital gains that have accrued only since 1972. Other countries, notably the United States, tax gains that have accrued since the acquisition of the asset. Thus, if you have owned an asset for many years — for example, a cottage or perhaps a work of art that you inherited when you were a child — and substantial gains have accrued since well before 1972, you may be better off disposing of the property before you leave Canada so you do not become liable for excess tax in your new country of residence. Of course, you should calculate what your ultimate tax liability might be compared with the tax that would be payable if you sell the asset before leaving Canada. If you are moving to a lower-tax jurisdiction, there may be little difference, or you actually may be better off holding on to the asset. However, you should also make careful note of the potential effect of any estate taxes that could become payable were you to die in that jurisdiction.

PUT YOUR INCOME SPLITTING PROGRAM IN HIGH GEAR

As we noted in Chapter 10, the income attribution rules cease to have any effect if you become a non-resident. Since you are no longer filing Canadian tax returns, tax cannot be attributed to you.

Just before you leave Canada, you might consider transferring a variety of assets into your spouse's name so as to more or less equalize your retirement incomes. Of course, you would only consider doing this if there were going to be a definite advantage in your new country of residence. If you are settling in the United States, there may not be much point, since you generally file a joint tax return, which acts to reduce your U.S. tax burden. However, this may not be the case if you are settling in another country. The message is clear. Do your homework before leaving Canada. If the rules in your new country of residence are anything like those in Canada, you will be very limited in how you can plan once you have established residence in the new country.

OWNERS OF PRIVATE CORPORATIONS

If you are the owner of a Canadian-controlled private corporation and you are planning to give up your Canadian residence, you should obtain competent professional advice well before you leave Canada. There is a variety of tax planning opportunities available for reducing the tax impact of leaving Canada. With the proper advice, you should be able to stop short of falling into one of the many tax holes that will open up as you contemplate dealing with your company and leaving Canada. In particular, you should ensure that your corporation meets the 24-month, 50 per cent test for purposes of qualifying for the $400,000 capital gains exemption on the disposition of shares in private Canadian corporations (see Chapter 12).

U.S. CITIZENS RETURNING TO THE UNITED STATES FROM CANADA

As a U.S. citizen working in Canada, you have been dealing with the two tax systems since the year you took up Canadian residence. Extricating yourself from the Canadian tax yoke in the near future may come as a welcome relief, but you should prepare yourself to do it properly and profitably.

Most of the comments made in this chapter also apply to U.S. citizens who have been working in Canada for the past few years, or many years, but upon retirement will be returning to the United States. For Canadian tax purposes, you will be treated exactly the same as any other Canadian resident who is emigrating to the United States. However, you may have a number of options open to you that are not available to persons who are not U.S. citizens. For example, many U.S. citizens working in Canada and preparing to return to the United States are employed by U.S. companies. You may have a variety of choices of how to be paid certain benefits. The list of considerations below is certainly not exhaustive. You are encouraged to get professional advice well before you wind up your stint in Canada and return to the United States.

- Will your pension be paid from the United States or from Canada or from both countries? Is there any advantage in arranging for a larger or smaller portion to be paid from one country or the other, ignoring the possible investment advantages of having it paid in one currency or the other?
- Do you have any choice over how to arrange for health care coverage, whether privately or through your employer or former employer, once you retire?
- How will you be taxed on other benefits of employment as you get close to retiring or after you retire? Should you exercise stock options now or after you leave Canada? What about U.S. stock options? How will the two regimes treat employee loans or any other benefits that you might continue to receive after you retire?
- If you are being transferred back to the United States for your last year or two of employment, remember that moving expenses incurred by you are not deductible from Canadian income in your last year of Canadian residence. You will be much better off being reimbursed for the expenses by your employer. First, though, be sure that the reimbursement will not generate any additional taxes in the United States. If it does, receive it while still a Canadian resident, in which case it will not be subject to tax.
- If you have been paying U.S. tax in the past on income earned inside your RRSP, you will definitely want to minimize any Canadian withholding on your RRSP, RRSP annuity income, or RRIF payments after you return to the United States. Generally, you will be better off retaining the plan in Canada and arranging for a retirement income. Collapsing the plan could subject you to a fairly healthy degree of double taxation.
- Timing your move back to the United States in the particular year could be important if you are likely to be subject to the U.S. alternative minimum tax. Generally, postponing the date to later in the year will prove beneficial, although then you could become subject to Canadian AMT. This would definitely not be

desirable, since you might not be in a position where you could file another Canadian return and claim any outstanding Canadian AMT credits that you have accumulated.

- If you have owned two homes in Canada for a number of years, you may, in some circumstances, be better off selling only one before you leave. The U.S. exemptions for a principal residence are not as generous as those in Canada, and the entire gain on the second residence will be fully taxable in the United States. Only limited foreign tax credits will be available in respect of this U.S. tax when you file a Canadian tax return for your year of departure.

  However, you can make an election under the Canada–United States tax treaty for the Canadian deemed disposition rules to apply for U.S. tax purposes. In this case, you would elect on all your Canadian property before you depart for the United States. Tax would be triggered in both countries, but the Canadian tax payable would be available as a credit against any U.S. taxes owing, and the cost base of the property would be stepped up so that much less tax would be owing on any eventual disposition.

- If you continue to own Canadian real estate after resuming U.S. residence, you should carefully consider any provincial laws that discriminate against foreign owners of real estate. For example, if you, as a U.S. resident, want to transfer ownership of your cottage to your children, who are all U.S. residents, there could be substantial land transfer, U.S. gift, or other types of taxes payable on the transaction in several provinces. Considering the cost of maintaining the property and the possibility of future taxes such as these, plus U.S. estate and gift taxes, it may make more economic sense to sell the property before you leave. Or you may be able to transfer the property into your children's names while still a Canadian resident and avoid certain provincial levies.

Chapter 18 —
Conclusion

You owe it to yourself and your family to begin planning for your retirement as soon as you possibly can. This includes making RRSP contributions early in your career. But primarily it means looking at the whole planning process once you are within five and preferably ten years of retiring. These are the years when your earnings are at a peak and you probably have the most flexibility to affect how you will spend the 20 or 30 years of retirement you and your spouse can look forward to. You have considerable negotiating power with your employer, or resources at your disposal if you are self-employed or run a business. You still have enough time to make good decisions and correct bad ones. Most importantly, you still can make up for all the planning you didn't do in previous years.

However, the closer you get to the day you actually retire, the fewer options you have to get the most out of your retirement years, at least financially. You simply can't do it all a month or two before you retire and expect to influence the quality of your retirement very much at all.

We cannot urge you too strongly to read, research your situation, consider all the possibilities that present themselves to you, and obtain quality professional advice in the areas that you feel need the helping hand of an expert.

Index